the best of thai
vegetarian
food

SISAMON KONGPAN

Sangdad Books Publishing Co.,Ltd.
Bangkok,Thailand

National Library of Thailand Cataloging in Publication Data
The Best of Thai Vegetarian Food.--5th ed.--Bangkok : Sangdad,
2005.
209 p.
1. Vegetarian Cookery. 2. Cookery, Thai.
I. Title.
641.5636
ISBN 974-7162-94-6

Sangdad Books
Published by Sangdad Publishing Co., Ltd.
320 Lat Phrao 94 (Town in Town)
Wangthonglang, Bangkok 10310, Thailand.
Tel. (662) 934-4413 Ext. 101-107
Fax: (662) 538-1499, 934-4415
e-mail : sdbooks@sangdad.com www.sangdad.com

First Published, November 1998
Second Published, February 2000
Third Published, November 2002
Fourth Published, December 2003
Fifth Published, July 2005

Director: Nidda Hongwiwat
Editor: Nidda Hongwiwat
Editor's Assistant: Obchery Imsabai
Photography: Sangdad Studio
Design: Samart Sudto
Lay out: Rungrudee Panichsri
Maketing Director: Pranee Pongpun
Production Director: Jiranan Tubniem

Preface

More and more people are turning to vegetarian foods nowadays due to growing interest in maintaining health and in the healing quality of meat-free diets ; this in addition to long standing religious reasons. This interest in vegetarian foods is present throughout the world—in the U.S.A., in Europe, in Asia and, of course, in Thailand.

Vegetarians differ in the degree to which animal products are restricted in their diets.

Vegans eat only fruits, vegetables, nuts, beans, sesame, cereals and consume neither eggs nor milk and other dairy products. Some also abstain from spices and certain spicy vegetables, such as garlic and onion.

A second type of vegetarian consumes milk and dairy products.

Thirdly, there are those who eat eggs and drink milk but do not consume other dairy products.

This book covers a wide range of recipes for meat-free dishes for all vegetarians as well as for non-vegetarians who wish to take good care of themselves and to enjoy cooking tasty and healthful food for themselves and for their loved ones.

Sisamon Kongpan
(Associate Dean)
Faculty of Home Economic,
Rajamangala Institute of Technology,
Bangkok, Thailand.

Introductions

Four major dietary components for vegetarians

1 Proteins build and maintain tissue and are also important in resistance to disease. Protein is found in peas and beans, especially soybeans, in mushrooms, unpolished rice, sesame, oilseeds, dehydrated soy protein extrudate, and also in vegetables.

2 Carbohydrates furnish energy to the body. Starchy foods such as unpolished rice, potato, taro, and sugar, especially brown sugar, are good sources.

3 Fats also supply our bodies with energy. We obtain fats from vegetable oil, milk, dairy products, nuts, peas, beans, sesame and other oilseeds.

4 Vitamins and minerals play important roles in the reactions essential for normal functioning of the body. Fresh vegetables, fruits, nuts, peas, beans, sesame and rice are important sources of these dietary components.

Main foods of vegetarians

1 Unpolished rice. If not available, cereal brans, cooked with ordinary polished rice or mixed in hot drinks can be used in its stead.

2 Beans and bean products, such as bean curd, soy sauce, formented soy beans, dehydrated soy protein extrudate.

3 Mushrooms.

4 Seeds, such as sesame, pumpkin seeds, sunflower seeds, and nuts.

5 Vegetables and fruits.

Water is also indispensable. We need at least eight glasses of pure water daily to refresh ourselves and to aid in elementation.

Main vegetarian foods and their nutrients

Unpolished rice and cereal brans contain 7-12% protein and more than twenty kinds of vitamins and minerals. The fiber in these foods is helpful in elimination. Fiber deficiency can cause diabetes, high blood-pressure, colon cancer, appendicitis, and varicose veins.

Soybean is a high-protein vegetable which can replace meat in the diet. Not only is it much less expensive than meat, but it also has certain nutrients in larger quantities than meat, such as unsaturated fat, which helps control cholesterol ; iron, which is essential to the blood, the liver, and the nerves ; and vitamin E.

Notes : The products from soybean are available in various forms, for instance, bean curd, dried soybean film, soybean milk, dehydrated soy protein extrudate, soy sauce, fermented soybean, fermented soybean paste, etc.

There are both coarse and fine kinds of dehydrated soy protein extrudate. The former can be used as chunks or slices of meat and the latter as ground or chopped meat. The white kind gives the appearance of pork or chicken meat while the brown type looks similar to beef. It must be soaked or scalded first for a sauteed dish but for soup or curry it can be used right away.

Mushrooms are also an excellent substitute for meat not only because they taste good but also because there is a large variety of mushrooms to choose from. Mushrooms contain about 3% protein and all essential amino acids. They are esspecially good for people who have heart, liver, or kidney disorders or high blood-pressure.

Seeds contain healthful fat and oil, 20% protein, vitamins A, C, and E, and minerals, especially selenium, which reduces the risk of cancer. Pumpkin seeds contain 20% protein, 46% fat and are extremely high in phosphorus.

Fruits and vegetables contain vitamins and minerals and also provide our bodies with fiber necessary for regular elimination. Vitamins and minerals in fruits and vegetables are essential for the healthfulness of our nerves, teeth and complexions. They are especially necessary for those who have diabetes and high blood-pressure.

Fiber-containing diets

As referred to herein, fiber means that part of plant material in the diet which is resistant to digestion by the secretions of the human gastrointestinal tract. Fiber-containing foods are fruits, vegetables and cereals, particularly in an unpolished form.

It has been observed that people whose diets are rish in fiber-containing foods have a lower incidence of appendicitis, hemorrhoids, diverticular disease, cardiovascular disease, and cancer of the colon than persons whose diets contain foods low in fiber. Scientific research has shown that fiber has a definite value in relieving constipation problems by increasing the water content of feces. It is very probable that fiber has a role in the prevention and treatment of diverticular disease and it probably reduce serum cholesterol, prevents a variety of disorders, such as hemorrhoids, varicose veins, ischemic heart disease, colon-rectal cancer, diabetes, appendicitis, obesity, gallstones, phlebitis, dental caries, irritable bowel, ulcerative colitis, and the harmful effects of some indigested toxic substances.

As vegetarian dishes are prepared mainly from vegetables, fruits and cereals, they, therefore, abound with fiber.

Ingredients

The basic rule for Thai cooking is that all ingredients should be ready before cooking begins. This means that each item has been cut into small or bite size to cook quickly. Here is a selective list of the commonly used ingredients :

Rice, khao jao, ข้าวเจ้า, the staple food in the central and southern parts of Thailand, is long-grained, nonglutinous rice. Uncooked grains are translucent ; when cooked, the rice is white and fluffy.

Glutinous rice, khao niao, ข้าวเหนียว, also known as sticky rice, is the mainstay of the diet in the northern and northeastern regions of the country and is used in confections in all regions. Uncooked grains are starchy white in color.

Palm sugar, nam tan pip, น้ำตาลปีบ, was originally made from the sap of the sugar, or palmyra, palm, *Borassus flabellifera,* called tan in Thai, which has a very rough trunk and large, fan-shapped leaves. Now it is generally made from the sap of coconut palms, and may be sold as coconut sugar. The sugar is a light golden-brown paste with a distinctive flavor and fragrance. It is put up in five-gallon kerosene cans, called pip in Thai.

Beancurd, tao hu, เต้าหู้, is made up salted and unsalted in solid and soft forms. The solid curd has a cheesy consistency and is sold in blocks about four inches square. The blocks of the unsalted curd are white while those of the salted, **yellow beancurd,** tao hu leuang, เต้าหู้เหลือง, are yellow on the outside and off-white inside. The solid curd is used in fried dishes. The **soft white beancurd,** tao hu khao chanit on, เต้าหู้ขาวชนิดอ่อน, is cut into bricks for sale and is used in soups.

Fermented soybeans, tao jiao, เต้าเจี้ยว, is a brew of soybeans and salt.

Soybean paste, tao jiao nam, เต้าเจี้ยวน้ำ, is a preparation made with fermented soybeans and flour.

Soy sauces, si-iu, ซีอิ๊ว, used in these recipes are of the Chinese, rather than the Japanese, type.

Light soy sauce, si-iu khao, ซีอิ๊วขาว, is a clear brown liquid used in much the same way that fish sauce is.

Dark soy sauce, si-iu dam, ซีอิ๊วดำ, is opaque, black, viscous, and sweet. It is mixture of soy sauce and molasses.

Mungbeans, thua khiao, ถั่วเขียว, are yellow beans with green shells. The shelled bean is used in sweets and the whole bean is sprouted, giving, **bean sprouts,** thua ngok, ถั่วงอก.

Kidney beans, thua dang leuang, ถั่วแดงหลวง, are big red beans, it looks like kidney.

Chillies, phrik, พริก, *Capsicum annuum,* of several varieties are available in Thailand. As they ripen, they change color from green to red and become hotter. Fully ripe fruits are dried in the sun to give **dried chillies,** phrik haeng, พริกแห้ง, and these are pounded for **ground dried chilli,** phrik pon, พริกป่น. **Hot chillies,** phrik-khi nu, พริกขี้หนู, are the hottest type and also the smallest, being only about a centimeter long.

Coconut, ma-phrao, มะพร้าว, *Cocos nucifera,* is found nearly everywhere people have settled in all parts of the country and its production is important to the economy. The use to coconut milk in curries is a hallmark of Thai cooking. The meat of ripe nuts is scraped either by hand or by machine. The grated coconut is placed in a basin and mixed with a certain amount of warm water. The coconut is then picked up in the hand, held over a second container, and squeezed to press out the **coconut milk,** ka-thi, กะทิ. A finemeshed strainer should be positioned below the hand during squeezing to catch any meat that falls. Many cooks add a little salt to the water or the milk.

Coconut cream, hua ka-thi, หัวกะทิ, can be obtained by mixing a little warm water with the grated coconut and collecting the required amount of cream on the first squeezing. Following this, water can be added again and the grated coconut can be squeezed a second and a third time to obtain a less rich milk, which is kept separate from the cream. Alternatively, the full amount of warm water may be mixed with the grated coconut. After squeezing, the liquid is allowed to stand for a time, and then the cream is skimmed from top with a spoon.

Garlic, kra-thiam, *กระเทียม*. Thai garlic has small cloves covered with a peel that is not tough. Its fragrance is stronger than that of large-cloved garlic. In making fried garlic, the peel is usually not removed entirely so that only the flesh remains. Some of the peel is left on the clove, for it is in the peel that the fragrance resides.

Garlic is an ingredient in all types of curries as well as of stir-fried and deep-fried dishes. The fragrance of garlic is one hallmark of Thai cooking.

Garlic is also used raw. Thin slices are mixed with chilli and fish sauce and used as a garnish by those who like their food hot.

Shallot, hom lek, *หอมเล็ก*, or hom daeng, *หอมแดง*, *Allium ascalonicum,* is the zesty small red onion favored in Thai cooking.

Yard-long beans, thua fak yao, *ถั่วฝักยาว*, have pods up to 60 cm long. These are eaten both fresh and cooked and are at their best when young and slender.

Kaffir lime, ma-krut, *มะกรูด*, Citrus hystrix, has green fruits with wrinkled skin. The rind and the leaves are used in cookery.

Mushrooms, het, *เห็ด*, of many types are available fresh. The common are the **rice straw mushroom,** het fang, *เห็ดฟาง*, the **angel mushroom,** het nang fa, *เห็ดนางฟ้า*, the **oyster mushroom,** het nang rom, *เห็ดนางรม*, the **abalone mushroom,** het pao heu, *เห็ดเป๋าฮื้อ*. These many types of commonly used mushroom could be substituted for one another in cooking, if necessary.

Ear mushroom, het hu nu, *เห็ดหูหนู*, is a dark greyish brown fungus that has a delightful crunchy texture.

Shiitake mushroom, het hom, *เห็ดหอม*, is available dried in the market.

Pandanus leaf, bai toei, *ใบเตย*, the leaves of a scented flower, which are used to add a fresh smell and bright green colour.

Coriander plant, phak chi, *ผักชี*, is used extensively as a flavouring, and as a garnish. The root is also used, often pounded with garlic and other ingredients to make a marinade. Leaf and root are bought complete.

Papaya, marakor, *มะละกอ*, a large green gourd-like fruit with soft yellow-orange flesh. When unripe and still green the fresh is used as vegetable.

Preserved vegetables, tang-chi, *ตั้งฉ่าย*, this is sliced vegetables, often found in vacuum-sealed packages from oriental stores. Use it in amounts, to add texture and flavour.

Ma-kheua phuang, *มะเขือพวง*, it one kind of eggplants, grow in cluster and, when yet unripe, look green, and look like large peas.

Contents

Snacks

Main Dishes

Khanom Jip (or Kiao Thot) Sai Phak
Steamed (or Fried) Won Ton with Vegetarian Filling

Luk Chin Thua Khiao
Mungbean Balls

Khanom Jip (or Kiao Thot) Sai Phak
Steamed (or Fried) Won Ton with Vegetarian Filling

Ingredients
80 won ton sheets, 1/4 cup diced onion
1/2 cup thinly sliced, soaked ear mushroom
1 cup peas or short lengths of green beans
1 cup diced carrot or diced pumpkin
1 tsp. chopped coriander root, 2 tbsp. fried garlic
1/4 tsp. pepper, 5 cloves garlic
1 tbsp. seasoning sauce, 1-2 tbsp. light soy sauce
1 tbsp. wheat flour, 2 tbsp. vegetable oil, 1 egg

Preparation
- Pound the coriander root, pepper, and garlic well in a mortar.
- Heat the oil in a frying pan. When it is hot, fry the garlic mixture until fragrant ; then, add the onion, mushrooms, peas (or beans), and pumpkin (or carrot) and stir fry until tender, seasoning with seasoning sauce and soy sauce. Separate the yolk of the egg from the white. Set the white aside for use in wrapping the won ton ; add the yolk to the pan ; then add the flour and mix thoroughly. When ready, remove from the pan and allow to cool.
- Place about 1 tsp. of the filling in the center of a won ton sheet and fold the sheet up by making small pleats all around the filling, sticking the sheet closed by dabbing it with a little of the egg white. Place the won ton on a lightly greased banana leaf or tray in a steamer and steam for about 15 minutes.
- After removing from the steamer, arrange on a plate, sprinkle with the fried garlic, and serve with light soy sauce, soy vinegar, or sliced chillies in vinegar.
- For Khanom Jip Sai Phak, place about 1 tsp. of the filling in the center of each won ton sheet, fold the sheet over the filling, wet the edges of the sheet with a little water,

(See p. 21)

Luk Chin Thua Khiao
Mungbean Balls

Ingredients
1 1/2 cups mashed, boiled, hulled mungbeans
3 coriander roots, well pounded
1/4 tsp. pepper
5 cloves garlic, well pounded
1 1/2 tsp. salt
2-3 tbsp. wheat flour
1 egg
1 tsp. vegetable oil

Preparation
- Mix all the ingredients and knead together until stiff. Taking one tablespoonful at a time, roll the dough into balls.
- Place the balls on a plate, put into a steamer in which the water is already boiling, and steam for five minutes. Then, remove the balls from the steamer and fry in plenty of oil. They may be served with chillies sauce, or catsup, or sweet and sour sauce. (See p. 37)

(From p. 20)

and then pinch the edges closed.
- Heat the 2 cups of oil in a frying pan. When it is hot, fry the won ton until crisp and golden brown ; then, remove from the pan and drain.
- Serve with chilli sauce or catsup.

Thot Man Khao Phot
Spicy Fried Corn Patties

Tao-hu Khao Thot
Fried Bean Curd

Thot Man Khao Phot
Spicy Fried Corn Patties

Ingredients
2 cups corn kernels (about 4 large ears)
1 egg
1/4 cup thinly sliced yard-long bean
1 tbsp. kaeng-khua chilli paste
2-3 tbsp. rice flour
2 tbsp. light soy sauce
1 tsp. salt
2 cups vegetable oil (for frying the patties)
3 tbsp. wheat flour (for flouring the patties)

Preparation
● Blend all ingredients with soy sauce and salt together and knead to a uniform texture.
● Form the dough into 1-inch balls, flatten slightly, flour with the wheat flour, and fry in hot oil. Fry 8-10 patties at a time. If too many patties are in the pan, a froth forms and the outside of the patties does not become crisp. Serve with relish.

Ingredients for chilli paste

5 dried chillies, soaked in hot water for 15 minutes and deseeded
3 tbsp. chopped shallots
2 tbsp. chopped garlic
1 tsp. chopped galangal
1 tbsp. chopped lemon grass
1 tsp. chopped kaffir lime rind
1 tsp. chopped coriander root
2 tsp. salt

Into a blender, put all ingredients and blend until well mixed. Keep the rest of chilli paste in the refrigerator.

Note
● Instead of kaeng-khun chilli paste, 1 tbsp. of well pounded coriander roots, and garlic may be used.

(See p. 25)

Tao-hu Khao Thot
Fried Bean Curd

Ingredients
4 cakes firm white bean curd
4 cups vegetable oil

Ingredients for the sauce
1/2 cup sugar
1/2 cup vinegar
3 tbsp. coarsely ground roasted peanuts
10 hot chillies, coarsely chopped
1 tsp. salt

Preparation
- Cut each cake of bean curd diagonally into four triangualar pieces. Heat the oil in wok, and when hot, fry the bean curd golden, and then remove it from the oil and drain.
- Mix the sugar, vinegar, and salt in a pot on low heat. Simmer until thickened, add the peanut and chilli, stir well, transfer to a bowl, and serve with the fried bean curd.

(From p. 24)

Relish

1/4 cup vinegar
1/4 cup water
1/4 cup sugar
1 tsp. salt
1 red spur chilli, well pounded
5 cucumbers, thinly sliced
1/4 cup roasted peanuts

Preparation
- Bring the vinegar, water, sugar, salt, and chilli to a boil and then allow to cool.
- Pound the peanuts well in a mortar and then mix with the syrup and add the cucumbers.

Tao-hu Sawt Sai
Fried Stuffed Bean Curd

Pheuk Thot
Fried Taro

Tao-hu Sawt Sai
Fried Stuffed Bean Curd

Ingredients
**3 cakes firm white bean curd, cut into triangular pieces
1 tbsp. chopped garlic
1/2 cup finely diced sweet potato
2 tsp. sugar
200 grams ricestraw mushrooms, chopped coarsely
1/2 an ear of corn, kerneled
1/2 carrot, finely diced
1 tbsp. arrowroot flour
2 cups vegetable oil
1 tbsp. light soy sauce
100 grams fine textured vegetable protein
1/2 onion, chopped finely
1/2 cup boiled soybeans
1 tbsp. wheat flour**

Preparation
- Cut hollows in the pieces of bean curd to receive the stuffing.
- Heat the oil in a wok, fry the garlic until fragrant, add the mushroom, and fry until just done. Add the protein carrot, potato, corn, soybeans, onion, sugar, soy sauce, and arrowroot flour and fry until done. Stuff the beancurd with this mixture and close the opening with a dough made from the wheat flour mixed with a little water. Deep fry until golden brown and serve with the sauce.

Pheuk Thot
Fried Taro

Ingredients
500 grams taro, peeled
1 tsp. pepper
1 cup coconut cream
2 tsp. salt
1 cup rice flour
1 cup wheat flour
1 tbsp. sugar
vegetable oil for frying

Preparation
- Slice the taro into long, thin sticks.
- Mix the wheat flour, rice flour, and coconut cream together, stirring to blend. Then, add salt, sugar, and pepper and stir to mix. Add the taro spears to the batter and stir in order to coat them well.
- Heat the oil in a wok. When it is hot, scoop about a tablespoonful of the batter into the oil, one at a time, forming regular size of batter balls. Deep fry until golden brown and remove to drain. Serve with sweet and sour sauce.
- Sweet and sour sauce, mix 1/2 cup sugar, 1/2 cup vinegar, and 1 tsp. salt in a pot on low heat. Simmer until thickened, add the peanut and chilli, stir well, transfer to a bowl.

Sateh
Tao-hu Babecue

Kha Kai Je
Vegetarian Drumsticks

Sateh
Tao-hu Babecue

Ingredients
4-6 cakes firm white bean curd
3 cups coconut milk
1 tbsp. curry powder
1 tsp. salt

Preparation
- Cut bean curd into strips of a size that can be conveniently impaled on sticks
- Mix the coconut milk with the curry powder and salt. Dip the dough on the sticks into this mixture and then broil over coals. Serve with peanut sauce and relish.

Peanut Sauce
5-6 lemon grass stalks, 7-8 slices of galangal
4 garlic bulbs, 4-5 shallots
20 dried spur chillies, 2 tbsp. light soy sauce
2 tbsp. palm sugar, 3 tbsp. tamarind juice
500 grams peanuts
500 grams grated coconut meat.

- Cut open the chillies, remove the seeds, and soak in water. Slice up the lemon grass and galangal. Peel the shallots and garlic. Place all of these and the soaked chilli in a mortar and pound thoroughly.
- Add 1 cup of warm water to the grated coconut meat and squeeze out 2 cup coconut cream.
- Roast the peanuts and then pound to grind thoroughly.
- Heat 1 cup coconut cream in a frying pan until some oil surfaces. Add the chilli mixture and stir to disperse. Add the soy sauce and cook a few moments ; then, add the peanuts, tamarind juice, and palm sugar
- Add coconut cream a little at a time, scraping and stirring the pan all the while. Do not allow the sauce to become too thick. The taste should be sour and salty and also somewhat sweet. Continue until all the coconut cream has been incorporated.

Relish
Mix 1/4 cup sugar with 1/4 cup vinegar and 1 tsp. salt and simmer for a while. Cut cucumbers, chillies and shallots into thin slices and add the liquid before serving.

Kha Kai Je
Vegetarian Drumsticks

Ingredients
1 large, thin sheet yuba
300 grams yuba
2 cups wheat flour
2 lemon grass stems
1 tbsp. coriander root
10 cloves garlic
1 tsp. pepper
1 tsp. salt
1 tbsp. palm sugar
1 cup tempura flour

Preparation
- Soak the 300 grams of yuba in water until softened.
- Pound the coriander root, garlic, and pepper well in a mortar.
- Mix the yuba with the pounded spices and then add the flour, salt, and palm sugar. Knead to mix thoroughly, trying to keep the mixture as dry as possible.
- Cut the sheet yuba into triangular pieces. Place some of the dough on each piece, and in the center of the dough, lay a lemon grass stem so that the base of the stem extends beyond the edge of the yuba sheet. Then, wrap the sheet yuba around the dough and the lemon grass stem, shaping it to look like a chicken drumstick.
- Place the drumsticks on a plate and steam for 15 minutes. Remove from the steamer, coat with the tempura flour and then fry until golden brown.
- Serve with chilli sauce.

Khanom Pang Na Thua Khiao
Fried Canapés with Mungbean Spread

Khanom Pang Na Het
Fried Canapés with Mushroom Spread

Khanom Pang Na Thua Khiao
Fried Canapés with Mungbean Spread

Ingredients
6 slices bread
1/2 cup finely pounded, hulled mungbeans
5 cloves garlic, 1 tsp. coriander root
1 tsp. salt,1/4 tsp. pepper
1 egg,1 tbsp. wheat flour
1 tbsp. seasoning sauce
3 cups vegetable oil for frying

Preparation
- Dry the bread in the sun or in a low oven until stiff and then cut each slice in quarters.
- Pound the garlic, coriander root, salt and pepper well in a mortar.
- Add the mungbean and pound to mix thoroughly ; then, transfer to a mixing bowl, add the egg, flour, and seasoning sauce, and knead until thoroughly mixed.
- Spread about 1 1/2 tsp. of this mixture on each slice of bread. The spread should be formed into a mound, thickest in the center and sloping smoothly to the edges of the bread.
- Heat the oil in a frying pan. When it is hot, place the bread in the oil spread side downward. When golden brown, remoe from the oil and drain. Serve hot with sauce.

Note
- Dried bread is crisper when fried and does not absorb much oil.

Sauce
1 red spur chilli, well pounded
1/2 cup vinegar,1/2 cup sugar, 1 tsp. salt
Mix the vinegar, sugar, and salt in a pot, simmer until the mixture starts to thicken, add the chilli, and continue cooking until thick enough to stick to the bread.

Khanom Pang Na Het
Fried Canapé with Mushroom Spread

Ingredients
1/2 cup finely pounded, hulled mungbeans
1/2 cup finely pounded corn kernels
1/2 cup finely chopped boiled mushroom
1 tbsp. wheat flour, 1 tbsp. seasoning sauce
1 tbsp. fine textured vegetable protein
1 tbsp. finely ground roasted peanuts
1 tsp. sugar
1 tbsp. chopped spring onion and coriander greens
1 tsp. finely chopped onion
1 tsp. well-pounded coriander root, garlic, and pepper
1/4 tsp. salt, 6 slices bread

Preparation
● Mix the flour, mungbean, corn, salt, sugar, seasoning sauce, mushroom, and pepper garlic coriander root mixture together well first and allow to stand.
● When ready to put the spread on the bread, mix in the onion, coriander and spring onion, peanut, and protein. If the spread is too dry, add a little of the water in which the mushrooms were boiled.

Applying the spread
● The bread should be thoroughly dried, by placing either in the sun or in a low oven. Dry bread will be crispy and will not absorb much oil. Apply the spread to the bread gently and not too thickly. It should be spread evenly. Heat oil in a wok, and when it is hot, fry the spread bread until very well done ; then, remove from the oil and drain.

Sauce
Mix 1/2 cup vinegar, 1/2 cup sugar, and 1 tsp. salt in a pot and simmer until the sugar begins to thicken. Add one well-pounded chilli, stir, and continue simmering until syrupy enough to stick when the bread is dipped in it.

Khanom Pang Sai Phak lae Sai Man kap Khao Phot
Sweet Potato and Pumpkin Filled Rolls / Potato and Corn Filled Rolls

Phak Chup Paeng Thot
Crisp Fried Vegetables

Khanom Pang Sai Phak lae Sai Man kap Khao Phot

Sweet Potato and Pumpkin Filled Rolls/ Potato and Corn Filled Rolls

Ingredients

**2 1/2 cups sifted wheat flour, 1/4 cup margarine
1 tsp. salt, 1 egg, beaten, 1/4 cup sugar
1 tbsp. fine-pelleted dry yeast, 1/2 cup milk**

Preparation

- Place the milk, sugar, margarine, and salt in a pot, heat gently with stirring until the sugar dissolves, and then transfer to a warm mixing bowl. Stir in 1/2 cup flour and then the yeast, and then the egg. Now, add the remaining flour a little at a time, kneading gently until the dough no longer sticks to the hands.
- Form the dough into a ball, place in a greased bowl, cover with a heavy cloth, and allow to rise about half an hour, or until the dough has doubled in size. Then, separate the dough into four portions and divide each of these into three so as to obtain 12 rolls of equal size.

Ingredients for filling

1 cup diced pumpkin (or 1 1/2 cups thinly sliced corn kernels)
1 cup diced sweet potato (or 1 cup diced boiled potato)
1/2 cup diced onion, 1 tbsp. seasoning sauce
1/2 tsp. salt, 2 tsp. light soy sauce
1/4 tsp. pepper, 2 tbsp. margarine

Preparation

Melt the margarine in a wok, add the onion and fry until fragrant : then, add the pumpkin (or corn kernels) and potato (or boiled potato) and fry over medium heat. Season with seasoning sauce, salt, soy sauce, and pepper, continue frying until dry, and then divide into 12 equal portions.

Filling the rolls

Spread the dough into circles with the center thicker than the edges. Place the filling in the center, and fold the edges

(See p. **41**)

Phak Chup Paeng Thot
Crisp Fried Vegetables

Ingredients
200 grams pumpkin, 1 sweet potato
200 grams angel mushrooms, 200 grams yard-long beans
500 grams grated coconut meat, 1/2 cup rice flour
1/2 cup wheat flour, 1/3 cup water, 3 cups oil

Spice Mixture
3 dried chillies, 1 tbsp. salt, 3 shallots, peeled, 3 garlic bulbs, peeled

Preparation
● Pound the spice mixture ingredients in a mortar until finely ground. Peel the potato and pumpkin and cut into sticks about an inch long and a centimeter thick.
● Mix 1/3 cup of water with the coconut and squeeze out 3/4 cup of coconut cream.
● Mix the flours with the coconut cream and then blend in the spice mixture.
● Wash the mushrooms, cut off any foreign matter around the bases, and slice the mushrooms in half.
● Separate the batter into four portions, one for each of the vegetables. Work the vegetables around in the batter so that each piece is coated.
● Heat the oil in a wok. When it is hot, dip up bite-sized portions of the vegetables and fry until golden brown ; then, remove from the oil and place on absorbent paper to drain. Serve hot as a snack.

(From p. 40)

up and over the filling to enclose it. Place the rolls in the compartments of a lightly greased muffin pan and allow to rise for about 15 minutes. Before baking, brush the rolls with the yolk of and egg mixed with one tablespoon of water. Bake at 350°F. for about 20 minutes. When the rolls are done, remove from the pan and place on a rack. Serve hot with tea.

Po-pia Thot
Fried Spring Rolls

Naem Sot
Sour and Spicy Wheat-Gluten Salad

Po-pia Thot
Fried Spring Rolls

Ingredients
**300 grams small spring-roll sheets
(keep wrapped up to prevent drying out)
25 grams mungbean noodles
3/4 cup mashed, boiled hulled mungbeans
1 cup shredded cabbage, 1/4 tsp. pepper
1 cup bean sprouts, root tips removed
1 1/2 tbsp. light soy sauce, 1 tbsp. chopped garlic
1 tbsp. vegetable oil for frying the garlic
2 tbsp. of a paste made by mixing flour and water and
then boiling to thicken
vegetable oil for frying the spring rolls**

Spring Roll Sauce
**1/4 cup vinegar, 1/4 cup sugar
1 tbsp. salt, 2 tsp. tapioca flour
1/2 half of a red spur chilli, seeds removed and well pounded**

Mix the vinegar, sugar, and salt in a pot and heat, stirring constantly until the sugar dissolves. When the mixture boils, add the chilli and the flour, stir until the flour is well incorporated, and remove from the heat.

Preparation
- Soak the noodles in water to soften them ; then, cut into short lengths and mix with the mashed mungbeans, cabbage, bean sprouts, pepper, and soy sauce.
- Fry the garlic in the 1 tbsp. of oil over low heat. When it yellows, add the noodle-mungbean mixture, and stir-fry until dry ; then, remove from the pan and allow to cool.
- Spread out a spring-roll sheet, place a heaping teaspoonful of filling in the middle, fold the end over the filling, roll to form a cylinder, and stick closed with a very small amount of the flour paste.
- Fry the spring rolls in hot oil over low heat until crisp and golden brown, drain, and serve with spring roll sauce, sweet basil (horapha), cucumbers, and lettuce.

Naem Sot
Sour and spicy Wheat-Gluten Salad

Ingredients

1/2 cup Shiangsai noodle soaked and cut into 1/2-cm to pieces
3/4 cup wheat gluten
500 grams well-mashed boiled hulled soybeans
1/2 cup roasted peanuts
2 tbsp. chopped garlic
1 cup sliced shallot
5 spring onions, sliced
1 cup sliced ginger
1 1/2 cups cooked rice
10 fried dried hot chillies
3 tbsp. fresh hot chillies
1 1/2 tbsp. pepper
1 1/2 tsp. salt
1 tbsp. lime juice

Preparation

● Pound the soybeans, garlic, pepper, rice, and salt thoroughly in a mortar and then allow to stand in the refrigerator for about three days to become sour.

● When the desired degree of sourness has been achieved, add the wheat gluten to the mixture and form into thin patties. Fry the patties until golden ; then, drain and crumble them.

● Add the ginger, shallot, peanuts, boiled Shiangsai noodle and the fresh chillies, and mix well. If not yet sour enough, add lime juice.

● Serve with lettuce, and for a hotter taste, with fried hot chillies, too.

Het Yawng
Mushroom Chips

Bai Horapha Thot Krop
Crisp Fried Basil Leaves

Het Yawng
Mushroom Chips

Ingredients
2000 grams oyster mushrooms
200 grams palm sugar
1 tbsp. pepper
50 grams chopped garlic
2 tbsp. light soy sauce
1 tbsp. salt
3 tbsp. water
vegetable oil for frying the mushrooms

Preparation
- Tear the mushrooms into pieces of uniform size and place in the sun to dry some. Pour oil into a wok until it is about half full and place on medium heat ; if the oil is not hot enough, the mushrooms will be oily ; if too hot, they will burn. Fry the mushrooms a handful at a time : they should have room to float as a single layer on the oil. Once the mushrooms have been placed in the oil, do not stir ; if you do, they will crinkle up. Watch them carefully, and when golden on one side, gently flip over to brown on the other ; then, remove and drain on absorbent paper.
- When all the mushrooms have been fried, dip the oil from the wok ; in the oil that remains fry the garlic, seasoned with a little pepper, until golden brown and then remove from the wok and set aside.
- Wipe the wok dry and put into it the palm sugar, soy sauce, salt, and water, and reduce the heat to low. Dip a piece of mushroom in the mixture in the wok and taste it.You may season additionally if necessary to get the right taste. Then, add the mushrooms and stir constantly with a wooden paddle to prevent sticking. The heat should be the lowest possible. Continue stirring for 10-15 minutes, taking care not to break the mushroom chips, and then add the fried garlic and pepper.

Bai Horapha Thot Krop
Crisp Fried Basil Leaves

Ingredients

2 cups sweet basil leaves (horapha)
2 garlic bulbs
10 hot chillies
1 tbsp. sugar
1 tbsp. light soy sauce
1 cup vegetable oil

Preparation

- Wash the sweet basil leaves and set the leaves aside to drain.
- Place the chillies and garlic in a mortar and pound to break them up ; they should not be pounded fine. Scoop the mixture from the mortar and put it on top of the sweet basil leaves.
- Heat the oil in a frying pan over high heat. When the oil is good and hot, place the sweetbasil leaves, chilli, and garlic in it. Use the spatula to keep the leaves in the center of the pan. When the leaves have become crisp, move the leaves to one side of the wok. Remove the oil all but about 1 tablespoonsful of oil from the wok, fry the chillies and garlic until fragrant. Add the soy sauce and sugar, stir fry crisp leaves for a while, until the leaves crisp again, dip onto a plate and serve hot.

THAI VEGETARIAN
FOOD

Sup Haeo Sai Khreuang Thet
Herb Cream of Water Chestnut Soup

50

Sup Khao Phot
Creamed Corn Soup

51

Sup Haeo Sai Khreuang Thet
Herb Cream of Water Chestnut Soup

Ingredients
1 1/2 cups sliced water chestnut
2 cups milk
1 bay leaf
3 holy basil leaves
2 tbsp. coarsely chopped celery
2 tbsp. margarine or butter
1 onion, thinly sliced
2 tbsp. wheat flour
3 cups vegetable stock
1 tsp. salt
1/4 tsp. pepper
1 shallot, coarsely chopped

Preparation
- Boil the milk, water chestnuts, bay leaf, holy basil leaves, and celery about 20 minutes.
- Fry the onion in the margarine. When tender, add the flour and stir to a smooth paste ; then, add the vegetable stock, and stir.
- Remove the bay leaf from the milk and add the fried onion in vegetable stock.
- Heat the milk, water chestnut, and onion for about five minutes. Remove all solid pieces, mash them thoroughly, return them to the milk, and simmer to a creamy consistency. Sprinkle with the salt, pepper, and chopped shallot dip into bowls, and serve.

Vegetable Stock
Ingredients
1 carrot, peeled and coarsely chopped
2 cellery plants, washed and chopped
1 Chinese radish, peeled and coarsely chopped
1 onion, coarsely choppped

(See p. 53)

Sup Khao Phot
Creamed Corn Soup

Ingredients
1/2 cup milk
3 ears corn
1 1/2 tsp. salt
1 1/2 tsp. seasoning sauce
1 1/2 tbsp. butter
1/2 an onion
1 1/2 tbsp. corn flour
1/2 tsp. pepper
1 cup vegetable stock

Preparation
● Slice the corn kernels from the cobs. Mince the onion.
● Stir fry the corn kernels and onion in the butter for about five minutes ; then, add the stock, milk and season to taste with salt, pepper, and seasoning sauce.
● Mix the corn flour with a little water and add some of the mixture to the corn to thicken it.

*(From p. **52**)*

2 tbsp. magarine
2 tsp. salt
1/2 tsp. pepper
2 bay leaves
10 cups water

Preparation
● Stir onion in the magarine, add the celery, carrot and radish. Stir fry until fragrant.
● Place the vegetable into a pot. Add the water, salt, pepper and bay leave. Put over a low heat for about an hour strain and retain the clear stock.

Sup Thua Leuang Phasom Khai
Steamed Soybean Filled Egg in Vegetable Soup

Sup Bai Toei
Padanus-Scented Pearl Barley and Mungbean with Coconut

Sup Thua Leuang Phasom Khai
Steamed Soybean Filled Egg in Vegetable Soup

Ingredients
2 eggs
1/2 cup soybeans boiled until soft and tender
1 tsp. pepper , 1 tsp. salt
1 tsp. seasoning sauce, 1 small boiled carrot
1 small boiled Chinese radish
1 Chinese mustard green
3 cups water or vegetable stock
1 tbsp. dark soy sauce

Preparation

- Beat the eggs enough to mingle the yolks and the whites, add the salt, 1/4 tsp. pepper, and seasoning sauce, and then gently beat to a uniform consistency, being careful not to raise any froth. Divide the beaten egg into two equal portions.

- Grease a square, 6 by 6 inch baking pan or a round baking pan. Pour one portion of egg into the pan, place in a steamer in which the water is already boiling, and steam over low heat for about five minutes. Open the steamer, sprinkle the boiled soybeans on the egg, covering the surface uniformly, and then gently pour the second portion of egg over the soybeans.

- Close the steamer and steam for about ten more minutes until the egg is done. Use a low heat ; otherwise, an unsightly foam will form. Remove the pan from the steamer, allow to cool, gently remove the egg from the pan, and cut into 1-inch squares, or cut into other shapes with a cookie cutter.

- Peel the carrot and radish, cut into discs about 1 cm thick. Cut the discs into squares and triangles or shape with cookie cutters.

- Boil the mustard green for three minutes in water to which salt has been added. Remove the greens, rinse in cold water, and cut into 1-inch lengths. Save the water

(See p. 57)

Sup Bai Toei
Pandanus-Scented Pearl Barley and Mungbean with Coconut

Ingredients

1/2 cup hulled mungbeans
10-15 pandanus leaves, 2 green coconuts
1/2 cup pearl barley, 1/2 cup tapioca flour
3/4 cup coconut cream, 1/2 tsp. salt

Preparation

- Soak the mungbeans in water for four to five hours and then steam until tender.
- Wash the pandanus leaves well,allow to drain,cut into thin slices, and squeeze to extract the juice. Strain the juice and set aside.
- Split the coconuts in half, collecting the coconut water. Scrape the coconut meat from the shell.
- Soak the pearl barley in water for four to five hours ; then, remove to a pot and add about three-quarters as much water as there is pearl barley. Boil until the pearl barley splits and swells.
- In a pot, blend the tapioca flour and the coconut water and pandanus-leaf juice well and then place on a high heat. Add the salt and stir constantly. When the mixture comes to a boil, add the mungbean and the pearl barley. Bring to a boil once again, add the coconut meat, and stir to mix thoroughly

(From p. 56)

in which the greens were boiled and add to your vegetable stock.
- Bring the water or vegetable stock to a boil, add the remaining 1/2 tsp. pepper, and the dark soy sauce, and stir. Add the carrot, radish, and mustard green and season further if necessary. When the soup returns to a boil, remove from the heat. Serve hot.

Sup Nam Nom Thua Leuang Sai Kiao Phak
Vegetarian Won Ton in Soybean Milk

Sup Phak
Vegetable Soup

Sup Nam Nom Thua Leuang Sai Kiao Phak.
Vegetarian Won Ton in Soybean Milk

Ingredients
2 cups soybean milk
2 cups water
1 tsp. salt
2 shallots, thinly sliced and fried until golden brown
1 tbsp. chopped celery
2 chinese mustard green plants
24 won ton sheets

Filling Ingredients
1 cake firm white bean curd, mashed
1 tbsp. vegetable oil
1/2 tbsp. corn flour
1/2 cup shredded carrot
1/2 cup shredded cabbage
1/2 cup bean sprouts
1 tsp. minced ginger
1 tbsp. light soy sauce
1 tsp. sugar
1 tsp. salt
1 tsp. sesame oil

Preparation
- Mix all the filling ingredients together.
- Place a spoonful of filling on a won ton sheet, fold by bringing two opposite corners of the sheet together so as to form a triangle ; then, fold the remaining two corners over on one another, firm with the hand, and touch a little water to the won ton sheet to keep it closed.
- Place the won ton in a pot of boiling water. When done, remove and drain.
- Wash the Chinese mustard green well. Cut into two-inch lengths, scald and set aside to drain.
- Mix the soy milk and the water in a pot, add the salt, heat to boiling, add the won ton, dip into small bowls lined with scalded mustard green, sprinkle with the celery or shallot or both, and serve.

Sup Phak
Vegetable Soup

Ingredients
1 carrot, peeled and cut into thin slices
300 grams unpeeled squash cut into one-inch squares
300 grams cabbage cut into bite-sized chunks
kernels sliced from one ear of sweet corn
any other vegetables you like
1 tbsp. light soy sauce
1 tsp. salt
4 cups vegetable stock

Preparation
● Heat the stock to boiling and add the squash. When it is tender, add the other vegetables.
● Add salt and light soy sauce to taste. The vegetables become more tender the longer you leave them in the hot water.

Vegetable Stock
Ingredients
2 Chinese radishes
1 celery plant
2 garlic plants
5-6 crushed pepper corns
1 tsp. salt
2 tsp. sugar
5 cups water

Preparation
● Peel the radishes, cut them into two-inch lengths, cut each length in half, and then place in a pot.
● Wash the garlic and celery plants. Cut them about halfway up the stems and then knot the plants together. Place them in the pot, add the water, pepper, salt, and sugar, and place on a low heat. Simmer until about 4 cups of liquid remain ; then, strain and retain the clear stock.

Sup Het
Mushroom Soup with Ginger

Sup Phak Rudu Ron
Summer Vegetable Soup

Sup Het
Mushroom Soup with Ginger

Ingredients
500 grams ricestraw mushrooms
200 grams ear mushrooms
200 grams abalone mushrooms
5-6 slices mature ginger
1 tsp. rock sugar
1 tbsp light soy sauce
1 coriander root
2 tbsp. arrowroot starch
6 cups vegetable stock

Preparation
- Wash the mushrooms and slice lengthwise.
- Place the ginger and coriander root in stock water and boil about five minutes. Remove the ginger and coriander root from the water, add the mushrooms, and boil about ten minutes. Add the arrowroot starch to chicken, add the rock sugar and light soy sauce to taste.

Vegetable Stock

Ingredients
1 big Chinese radish
7 cups water
1 tsp. salt
3 celery plants
5 pepper corns

Preparation
- Wash the radish, peel and cut them into chunks, then place in a pot.
- Add the water and heat to boiling.
- Add the celery, pepper and salt. Lower the heat and simmer for about 30 minutes.

Sup Phak Rudu Ron
Summer Vegetable Soup

Ingredients

2 cups water
4 peeled potatoes
1 tsp. salt
1/2 tsp. pepper
2 tbsp. margarine
6 spring onions
6 peeled carrots
10 yard-long beans
1/2 cup sweet peas

Preparation

- Cut the potatoes into quarters lengthwise and then cut each quarter in half. Wash the spring onions, cut off the roots, and cut into 1-inch lengths. Cut the yard-long beans into 1-inch sections. Cut carrots into 1-cm slices lengthwise and then cut each slice in half.
- Place the water in a pot with a capacity of ten cups and heat to boiling. Then, add the potato, reduce the heat to a simmer, and add the salt, pepper, and margarine. Add the peas and carrot and cook until the vegetables are tender. Then, add the yard-long beans and spring onions and stir well.

Note

- If you prefer cream soup, mix 2 tbsp. of wheat flour and 3 tbsp. of water to obtain a uniform paste. Remove the pot from the heat, add the flour paste, stir well, return the pot to the heat until the flour is incorporated into the soup, and then dip into bowls and serve.

Sup Phakkat Khaopli kap Tao-hu Khao
Chinese Cabbage, Bean Curd, and Mushroom Soup

Khao Tom Khao Khlawng
Brown Rice Porridge with Gluten Balls

Sup Phakkat Khaopli kap Tao-hu Khao

Chinese Cabbage, Bean Curd, and Mushroom Soup

Ingredients

2 cakes firm white bean curd
1 large Chinese cabbage
10 ricestraw mushrooms
5 cups water
2 tbsp. light soy sauce
1 tsp. salt
1 tsp. vinegar
1/4 tsp. pepper
1 tsp. sugar
1 spring onion, cut into 1-inch lengths

Preparation

- Cut the bean curd into 2-cm squares. Wash the cabbage, separate into leaves, cut each leaf in half lengthwise, and then cut each half into 1-inch sections. Wash and clean the mushrooms and cut lengthwise into quarters.
- Place the water, soy sauce, salt, vinegar, and sugar in a pot and heat to boiling. Add the cabbage and mushrooms. When they have become tender, add the bean curd. When the cabbage breaks up easily, remove from heat, dip into bowls, and sprinkle with the spring onion.

Khao Tom Khao Khlawng
Brown Rice Porridge with Gluten Balls

Ingredients

2 cups brown rice
10 cups water
2 tbsp. dried preserved vegetables (tang-chai)
1 small branch young ginger, minced
4-5 ricestraw mushrooms, finely chopped
1/2 onion, finely chopped
1 tbsp. wheat gluten
1-2 coriander roots
4-5 cloves garlic
2 tbsp. light soy sauce
1 tsp. pepper
2 tbsp. chopped spring onions
2 tbsp. chopped coriander greens

Preparation

- Wash and clean the rice, and then rinse twice.
- Put the rice in a pot, add the water, and boil until mushy.
- Boil the mushroom until done, remove from the water, mix with the onion and knead together.
- Pound the coriander root and garlic in a mortar until finely ground and then mix with the mushroom and onion. Add the wheat gluten, pepper, and a little soy sauce and knead to mix. Take one-teaspoonful portions of this dough, form into balls, arrange on a plate, and place in a steamer in which the water is boiling until done.
- Add the minced ginger to the boiled rice, add the dried preserved vegetables and then add the gluten balls. Season with additional soy sauce if necessary. Sprinkle with chopped spring onion and coriander greens or with fried garlic before serving.

Krapho Pla Je
Quail's Egg and Bamboo Shot Soup

Khao Tom Sam Si
Colorful Rice Porridge

Krapho Pla Je
Quail's Egg and Bamboo Shoot Soup

Ingredients
10 boiled, peeled quail's eggs
1 cup bamboo shoot (cut into 1 1/2-inch-long pieces
about the diameter of a pencil)
1 cup ear mushrooms
4 cups vegetable stock (See p. 61)
1 tsp. salt
2 tbsp. light soy sauce
1 tbsp. dark soy sauce
1 boiled carrot
1/2 tsp. pepper
2 coriander plants
1 spring onion

Preparation
● Wash the mushrooms and remove the roots and any dirt attached.
● Heat the vegetable stock in a pot and add the mushrooms, bamboo shoot, salt, light and dark soy sauces, and pepper.
● Peel the carrot, cut in half lengthwise, cut each half into 1/2-cm-thick slices, and add to the pot.
● Wash the coriander and spring onion and chop coarsely.
● Add the eggs to the pot. Add the coriander and spring onion, remove from the heat, dip into bowls, and serve.

Khao Tom Sam Si
Colorful Rice Porridge

Ingredients
5 cups cooked rice
8 cups water
1/2 cup diced pumpkin
1 cup boiled red kidney beans
1 cup boiled mungbeans
3 tbsp. light soy sauce
1 tsp. salt
2 tbsp. dried preserved vegetables (tang-chai)
2 tbsp. vegetable oil
3 cloves garlic, crushed and chopped

Preparation
- Fry the garlic in the oil until fragrant ; then, add the kidney beans, mungbeans, and pumpkin and fry a few moments with stirring and turning.
- Heat the water, add the rice, and the fried beans seasoning with soy sauce, salt, and dried preserved vegetables. Serve hot.

Khao Phat Sapparot
Pineapple Fried Rice

Khao Phat Si-iu
Vegetarian Fried Rice

Khao Phat Sapparot
Pineapple Fried Rice

Ingredients
1 pineapple, cut its meat into small dice-shapes
2 cups ricestraw mushrooms cut in half
2 cups onion cut into small dice-shapes
2 cups tomato cut into small dice-shapes
2 cups yard-long bean chopped into 1/2-inch lengths
1 cup coarse textured vegetable protein
1/2 cup well-pounded mature ginger
8 cups cooked rice
1 tbsp. chopped garlic
1 tsp. pepper
1 tsp. palm sugar
1 tbsp. fermented soy beans
1 tbsp. light soy sauce

Preparation
- Scald the beans in boiling water and set aside.
- Fry the garlic in oil. When it begins to yellow, add the mushrooms and vegetable protein and fry, stirring and turning regularly.
- Season to taste with the ginger, fermented soybeans, light soy sauce, sugar, and pepper ; then, add the pineapple and then the rice, the onions, and the tomatoes, stirring and turning to mix and to prevent sticking. Add the beans, mix in well, remove from the heat, and serve.

Khao Phat Si-iu
Vegetarian Fried Rice

Ingredients

3 cups cooked rice
1/4 cup boiled corn kernels
1/2 cup diced pineapple
1/4 cup diced tomato
1/2 cup boiled red kidney beans
1 tbsp. coarsely chopped garlic
1/4 cup vegetable oil
1 tbsp. light soy sauce
1/2 tsp. salt
1/4 tsp. pepper

Preparation

- Heat the oil in a wok, and when hot, fry the garlic until fragrant ; then, add the beans, rice, and corn, and stir fry until the rice dries to the degree desired. Then, add the tomato and pineapple.
- Season to taste with soy sauce, salt, and pepper, stir thoroughly, dip onto plates, and serve with spring onions, sliced cucumber, and other vegetables.

Khao Rat Na Tao-hu Song Khreuang
Bean Curd and Vegetables in Sauce on Rice

Khao Phat Khamin
Savory Fried Rice

Khao Rat Na Tao-hu Song Khreuang
Bean Curd and Vegetables in Sauce on Rice

Ingredients
5 cups cooked rice
300 grams chinese kale
200 grams ricestraw mushrooms
1 carrot
1 cake firm white bean curd
3 cups water
2 tbsp. vegetable oil
1 tbsp. chopped garlic
2 tbsp. seasoning sauce
1-2 tbsp. light soy sauce
1/2 tsp. pepper, 1 tbsp. sugar
1 tbsp. tapioca flour mixed with 1/2 cup water
1-2 tbsp. of spur chillies sliced into rings mixed with vineger

Preparation
- Wash the kale. Peel off the tough outer portion of the larger stems and slice diagonally into pieces about an inch long. Cut tender small stems in half lengthwise. Cut the leaves into strips about an inch wide.
- Bring the water to a boil, add 1 tsp. of salt, immerse the kale stems in the water. When done, remove the stems, immerse the leaves until done. Save the water for use as vegetable stock.
- Clean and wash the mushrooms and cut in half lengthwise.
- Boil the carrot whole. When done, peel it and cut into 1/4-inch-thick slices.
- Wash the bean curd and cut into 1-cm squares.
- Fry the garlic in the oil until fragrant. Add the bean curd, and when this has yellowed, the mushrooms. Add the vegetable stock and the seasoning sauce, soy sauce, pepper, and sugar. When the sauce comes to a boil, add the kale, carrot, and the flour and water batter. Stir to mix well, season further if necessary, and remove from heat.

(See p. 81)

Khao Phat Khamin
Savary Fried Rice

Ingredients

2 cups diced sweet potato
2 cups diced taro
2 cups diced pumpkin
100 grams coarse textured vegetable protein
200 grams ricestraw mushrooms, cut in half
2 cups diced onion
500 grams diced tomato
300 grams spring onions cut into 1 1/2-inch lenghts
15 cups cooked rice
1 tbsp. curry powder
1 1/2 tbsp. turmeric powder
1 tbsp. chopped garlic
1 tbsp. palm sugar
4 tbsp. light soy sauce
1 tsp. pepper

Preparation

- Fry the garlic. When golden, add first the vegetable protein, then the mushrooms, then the taro, then the potato and pumpkin, turning and stirring after each addition. When about done, add soy sauce and palm sugar to taste.

- Add curry powder, pepper, and turmeric, stir to mix well, and then add the rice, stirring and turning regularly. Then, add the onion and tomato, mix in and, add soy sauce and other seasonings as needed. When ready, add the spring onion, remove from heat, and serve with sliced cucumbers.

(From p. 80)

- Place portions of rice on plates and spoon the sauce over the rice. This sauce is also good with egg noodles or with rice noodles.

Kuai -tiao Lot
Steamed Rice Noodle Rolls

Kuai-tiao Phat Thai Sai Thua Daeng
Stir-Fried Noodles and Kidney Beans

83

Kuai-tiao Lot
Steamed Rice Noodle Rolls

Ingredients
1000 grams rice noodle sheets
500 grams bean sprouts
4 cakes firm white bean curd
500 grams ricestraw mushrooms
200 grams ear mushrooms
500 grams onions, 300 grams garlic
1 tsp. pepper, 1 tbsp. palm sugar
1 tsp. salt, 1 tbsp. dark soy sauce
1 tbsp. light soy sauce, 4 tbsp. vegetable oil
5 coriander roots, 1 tbsp. five-spices powder
200 grams chopped pickled dried Chinese radish

Preparation
- Pound the coriander roots, 100 grams garlic, and pepper well in a mortar.
- Wash the mushrooms and chop into small pieces.
- Cut the bean curd into long, thin slivers, slice up the onions from top to bottom and then slice up cross-ways
- Fry the pounded coriander root-garlic-pepper mixture in oil until golden. Add the dark soy sauce, palm sugar, five-spices powder, and salt. When fragrant, add the bean curd, mushrooms, and onions, and mix well. There should not be too much liquid.
- Chop the remaining garlic and then fry in oil until golden, for sprinkling over the rice noodle rolls. Wash the bean sprouts, scald in boiling water, and set aside.
- Place some of the filling on a noodle sheet and arrange in an elongated pile. Fold the sheet over each end of the pile and then roll up the filling in the sheet. Place the rolls on a dish and steam until they are hot.
- Dip the rolls onto plate, and then cut into bite-sized pieces. Sprinkle with fried garlic, dark soy sauce, chillies and garlic in vinegar, and coriander leaves.
- The dark soy sauce should be diluted with a little water

(See p. 85)

Kuai-tiao Phat Thai Sai Thua Daeng
Stir-Fried Noodles and Kidney Beans

Ingredients
300 grams narrow rice noodles
1 cup boiled kidney beans
1/2 cup roasted peanuts
2 tbsp. light soy sauce
1 cake firm yellow bean curd
1/4 cup vegetable oil
1 tbsp. minced garlic
2 tbsp. sugar, 4 tbsp. vinegar
1 cup water, 2 cups bean sprouts
5-10 Chinese chives, cut into lengths
150 grams lettuce

Preparation
- Pound the peanuts in a mortar until coarsely ground.
- Cut the bean curd into small, rectangular pieces.
- Heat the oil in a wok, and when hot, add the garlic and fry until golden. Add the noodles, beans, and bean curd, season to taste with soy sauce, sugar, and vinegar, and add the water.
- Stir fry until the noodles are tender ; then, add the bean sprouts and Chinese chives, stir well, and remove from the wok. Serve with fresh bean sprouts, lettuce and other vegetables, as well as sugar, pepper, and wedges of lime.

*(From p. **84**)*

and then mixed with a little palm sugar.
- Chillies and garlic in vinegar is prepared by placing red and yellow spur chillies and peeled garlic cloves in a frying pan without oil and pan roasting with constant turning for a short time. This eliminates unpleasant odors. The chillies and garlic are then pounded well in a mortar with the addition of a little salt and then mixed with vinegar.

Phat Thai Rai Sen
Stir-Fried Bean Curd and Pickled Radish

Mi-sua Mangsawirat
Stir-Fried Mi-sua Noodles

Phat Thai Rai Sen
Stir-Fried Bean Curd and Pickled Radish

Ingredients
1 cake firm yellow bean curd
50 grams chopped salty, dried pickled Chinese radish
1/4 cup ground roasted peanut
1 tsp. ground dried chilli
1 tbsp. palm sugar
2 tbsp. light soy sauce
3 tbsp. tamarind juice
1/4 cup vegetable oil
2 eggs
1 tbsp. chopped garlic
1 cup bean sprouts
Chinese chive leaf, cut into short lenghts
lime

Preparation
- Heat three tablespoonsful of oil in a wok. When hot, add the garlic and fry until golden ; then, add the bean curd and fry. Add the radish, chilli, peanut, sugar, soy sauce, and tamarind juice, stir, and season additionally if desired.
- Add the bean sprouts, and Chinese chives and stir ; then, move the contents of the wok to one side. Add a little more oil, break the eggs into the wok, and with the spatula, spread them around the wok. Now, move the vegetables back to the middle, and stir and turn to mix the egg and vegetables thoroughly. When the egg has reached the desired degree of firmness, dip up from the wok and serve with wedges of lime, sugar and ground dried chilli.

Mi-sua Mangsawirat
Stir-Fried Mi-sua Noodles

Ingredients
300 grams mi-sua noodles
3-4 shiitake mushrooms
1/4 head cabbage
1 spring onion
1/2 tsp. pepper
1 tbsp. chopped garlic
3 tbsp. vegetable oil
3 tbsp. light soy sauce

Preparation
- Cook the noodles in boiling water until tender all the way through. Drain and wash with cold water, and then set aside.
- Soak the mushrooms in water until softened and then cut into bite-sized pieces. Retain the water in which the mushrooms were soaked.
- Cut the cabbage into large slices, cut the spring onion into sections, and then wash thoroughly and set aside.
- Heat the oil in a wok. When hot, fry the garlic until fragrant ; then, add the mushrooms and then the cabbage, the soy sauce, and 4-5 tablespoonsful of the water in which the mushrooms were soaked. Stir fry until the vegetables are done ; then add the noodles, stir and turn to mix well, and then serve.

Kuai-tiao Phat Khi Mao
Spicy Stir-Fried Noodles

Phat Makkaroni
Stir-Fried Macraroni

Kuai-tiao Phat Khi Mao
Spicy Stir-Fried Noodles

Ingredients
500 grams broad rice noodles
1 tsp. dark soy sauce
1 cup coarsely chopped mushroom
3 yellow chillies
10 cloves garlic
1/4 cup holy basil leaves
2 red spur chillies, sliced diagonally
1/4 cup vegetable oil
1 tsp. sugar
1 tbsp. light soy sauce
1/2 tsp. salt

Preparation

- Separate the noodles ; then, add the dark soy sauce and work the noodles around so that they become coated with the sauce.

- Pound the yellow chillies, garlic, and salt in a mortar until ground and thoroughly mixed.

- Heat the oil in a wok, add the chilli mixture and fry until fragrant ; then, add the mushrooms and stir fry until tender. Now, add the spur chilli and the holy basil and stir well.

- Add the noodles, stir, and season additionally as desired with light soy sauce and sugar. Continue stirring until the noodles are heated and everything is mixed well ; then dip onto plates and serve hot.

Phat Makkaroni
Stir-Fried Macaroni

Ingredients

1 cup macaroni
4 tomatoes, thinly sliced
100 grams mushrooms with caps expanded, sliced
50 grams baby corn, cut in half lengthwise and across
50 grams cauliflower, sliced
1/4 onion, sliced
50 grams carrot, sliced into small pieces
2 spring onion stems (remove the leaves as they
become soggy) cut into short lengths
1/2 cup coarse textured vegetable protein
1/4 cup vegetable oil

Sauce

2 tbsp. catsup
1 tbsp. seasoning sauce
1 tbsp. vinegar
1 tbsp. sugar
1/2 tsp. pepper
1/2 tsp. salt

Preparation

- Mix the ingredients for the sauce, seasoning to taste.
- Boil water, add some salt, and cook the macaroni until it expands and the color changes. Then, remove the macaroni, place in cold water, and set aside.
- Place the vegetable protein in a cup, splash with the seasoning sauce, add some hot water, cover, and set aside.
- Heat oil in a wok, add the baby corn, cauliflower, onion, carrot, mushrooms, and the soaked protein and stir to mix well. Add the macaroni and cook with turning and stirring until the oil penetrates it.
- Add some of the sauce and stir.
- Add the tomatoes and onions and then the remainder of the sauce and stir.
- Sprinkle on the spring onion and then remove from the pan.

Khao Soi
Egg Noodles in Spicy Coconut Soup

Bajang
Glutenous Rice with Penuts and Mushroom

Khao Soi
Egg Noodles in Spicy Coconut Soup

Ingredients

**500 grams unexpanded ricestraw mushrooms
washed and cut in half
1/2 bag coarse textured vegetable protein
1000 grams egg noodles
300 grams thinly sliced shallot
1000 grams grated coconut meat
300 grams chopped pickled Chinese mustard green
200 grams thinly sliced spring onion
5 limes, 2 tbsp. light soy sauce
1 tbsp. dark soy sauce, 1 tbsp. salt**

Spice mixture
**5 disc-shaped sliced galangal
2 stems lemon grass, sliced, 5 shallots
5 garlic bulbs, 10 dried spur chillies
5 coriander roots, 1 tsp. coriander seed
1/4 tsp. cumin, 1 tbsp. curry powder
50 grams ginger, 1 tbsp. turmeric powder**

Preparation

- Pound the spice mixture ingredients in a mortar until finely ground and thoroughly mixed. Heat 1/4 tbsp. of oil in a wok, fry the spice mixture until fragrant, and then remove and set aside.

- Mix the coconut with 4 cups water, and squeeze out 6 cups of coconut milk. Skim off one cup of coconut cream, and place the rest of the coconut milk in a wok and bring to a boil. Add the spice mixture, stir to disperse, and then add the mushrooms, the vegetable protein, light and dark soy sauces, and salt. When the mixture comes to a boil, add the coconut cream and place on a low heat to keep hot.

- Cook three-fourths of the noodles by immersing in boiling water ; deep fry the remainder.

- In serving, place some of the boiled noodles in a bowl,

*(See p. **97**)*

Bajang
Glutenous Rice with Peanuts and Mushroom

Ingredients

3 cups glutenous rice
1 1/2 cup boiled peanuts
1/2 cup blanched coarse textured vegetable protein
2-3 shiitake mushrooms, soaked and sliced
1 tsp. pepper, 1 tsp. salt
2-3 coriander roots, pounded fine

Preparation

- Soak the rice overnight. Drain it just before you are ready to use it.
- Mix the protein, peanuts, mushrooms, pepper, salt, and coriander root together.
- Heat a little oil in a wok, add the rice and other ingredients and stir fry until fragrant. Now, transfer to a plate and place in a steamer in which the water is already boiling for half an hour or until the rice is cooked.
- If you use bamboo leaves as wrappers, soak the leaves until flexible. Place two leaves together to make a double layer, form into a cone, press about two tablespoonsful of rice into the point, add some of the lotus seed mixture and then a little more rice, press to firm, close the leaf wrapper and tie securely, and then boil for about one hour.

(From p. 96)

add some shallot, pickled mustard green, and spring onion, dip on some of the soup, and top with some of the fried noodles. Served with wedges of lime.

Khao Man
Rice Cooked in Coconut Milk

Som Tam
Shredded Papaya Salad

Khao Man
Rice Cooked in Coconut Milk

Ingredients
2 cups uncooked rice
500 grams grated coconut meat
1 tsp. salt, 2 tsp. sugar

Preparation

- Mix the coconut with some water and squeeze to obtain 3 1/2 cups of coconut milk. Add the salt and sugar and stir until dissolved.
- Wash the rice and then drain it.
- Heat the coconut milk to a boil ; then, add the rice and cover the pot. When the coconut milk returns to boiling, reduce the heat and stir regularly to prevent sticking. Continue cooking until no liquid remains ; then, remove from heat and allow the rice to stand for a time in the covered pot so that it becomes thoroughly done.

Som Tam
Shredded Papaya Salad

Ingredients
3 cups shredded green papaya
3 tbsp. ground roasted peanuts
5 cloves garlic
3 dried chillies
5 cherry tomatoes, cut into quarters lengthwise
3 tbsp. lime juice
1 tbsp. palm sugar
2 tbsp. tamarind juice
1 tbsp. light soy sauce
1 tsp. salt
yard-long beans
swamp cabbage tips
cabbage

Preparation

- Peel a green papaya, wash it, and then cut into long thin shreds.
- Cut open the chillies, remove the seeds, and soak the skins in water for a short time. Remove the skins from the water, squeeze dry, pound well in a mortar with garlic and then mix in the shredded papaya, peanuts, tomatoes, and 1/2 cup yard-long bean, seasoning to taste with lime juice, soy sauce, salt, tamarind juice, and palm sugar.
- Serve with vegetables such as swamp cabbage tips, yard-long beans, and cabbage.

Salat Fak Thong
Pumpkin Salad

Salat Phonlamai
Fruit Salad

Salat Fak Thong
Pumpkin Salad

Ingredients
1/2 head cabbage, thinly sliced
1 onion
1 boiled kidney beans
1 potato or sweet potato
1 cake firm white bean curd
4 cucumbers
3 tomatoes

Dressing
1000 grams grated coconut meat
300 grams ground roasted peanuts
500 grams pumpkin, 2 tbsp. palm sugar
1 tbsp. salt, 10 shallots
5 garlic bulbs, 5 red spur chillies
7 coriander roots, 1/4 cup tamarind juice
1 tbsp. curry powder, 1 tbsp. light soy sauce

Preparation
- Squeeze the coconut to obtain 4 cups of coconut milk. Skim off the coconut cream and rcserve separately.
- Wash and peel the pumpkin, cut into chunks, steam until done, allow to cool, and then mash.
- Cut the garlic and shallots into thin slices and fry until they begin to turn yellow.
- Pound the chilli and coriander roots well in a mortar ; then, add the fried garlic and shallot and pound until thoroughly ground and mixed.
- Heat the coconut cream. When oil surfaces, add the chilli mixture and the curry powder and cook until fragrant, stirring to disperse. Add the remaining coconut milk, the mashed pumpkin, and the peanuts, seasoning with palm sugar, salt, tamarind juice, and soy sauce to taste. Simmer over a low heat for about ten minutes.
- Wash and peel the potatoes and soak for a while in water. Then, slice into thin discs and fry in hot oil until

(See p. 105)

Salat Phonlamai
Fruit Salad

Ingredients
1/2 cup 1-cm chunks of firm, ripe papaya
1/4 cup firm, ripe banana slices dipped in lime juice
1/2 cup 1-cm chunks of jujube (or tangerine sections)
1/4 cup grape
1 lettuce plant

Dressing
1/4 cup sugar
1 tsp. salt
1/4 tsp. mustard powder
1/4 cup vinegar
1/2 cup vegetable oil
1 tbsp. finely chopped onion
1 tbsp. ground papaya seed

Preparation
- Stir the oil and sugar together, add the vinegar, salt, mustard, onion, and papaya seed, and blend together.
- Mix the dressing with the prepared fruit and then chill.
- At mealtime, place one leaf of lettuce on a small plate, scoop the fruit and dressing onto the lettuce, and serve as the first course.

(From p. 104)

crisp and golden. Drain, and if not used immediately, store in a tightly closed container.
- Fry the bean curd until golden and then cut into thin slices.
- Place lettuce and slices of bean curd, tomato, cucumber, and onion on a platter, spoon the salad dressing over the salad, and top with fried potato.

Salat Khaek
Salad with Spicy Thick Dressing

Yam Mamuang kap Het Nang Fa
Spicy Mango and Mushroom Salad

107

Salat Khaek
Salad with Spicy Thick Dressing

Ingredients
2 lettuce plants, 1 onion
10 cucumbers, 10 small tomatoes
100 grams bean sprouts, 3 hard-boiled eggs
1 cake firm white bean curd
1 potato or sweet potato

Dressing
1/4 cup boiled hulled mungbeans
300 grams grated coconut meat
3 dried spur chillies, 1 tsp. thinly sliced roasted galangal, 2-3 tsp. salt
2 tbsp. palm sugar, 6 shallots
5 pepper corns, 2 tbsp. roasted peanuts
2 tbsp. tamarind juice, 1 tsp. curry powder

Preparation

- Cut open the chillies, remove the seeds, and soak in water for a time.
- In a mortar, pound the chillies, galangal and pepper until thoroughly ground and mixed.
- Add the shallots and pound to paste. Add the peanuts and mungbeans and pound to mix thoroughly.
- To the coconut, add 1 1/4 cups warm water and squeeze out 2 cups of coconut milk. Transfer to a frying pan, and heat to boiling over a low medium heat, stirring constantly.
- When some oil has surfaced, add the chilli paste, stir, and cook a few moments until fragrant ; then, add salt, sugar, and tamarind juice and the curry powder. When the taste is satisfactorily salty, sweet, and sour, remove from heat.
- Cut the potato and the bean curd into thin slices and fry until crisp.
- Wash the vegetables and allow to drain lettuce-cut into 2-inch lengths, onion - cut across into 1/2-cm thick slices, cucumber - cut across into 1/2-cm thick slices, tomatoes

(See p. 109)

Yam Mamuang kap Het Nang Fa
Spicy Mango and Mushroom Salad

Ingredients
1 tart green eating mango
300 grams angel mushrooms
10 hot chillies sliced thin
3-4 shallots sliced thin
2 spring onions sliced thin
2 tbsp. sugar
1/4 tsp. salt
1 1/2 tbsp. light soy sauce
1 lettuce plant

Preparation
- Peel the mango, wash to remove any sap, cut the flesh from the seed in chunks, and then cut into shreds. It is not necessary to squeeze any of the liquid from the mango.
- Wash the mushrooms, remove the bases, tear into bite-sized pieces, scald in boiling water, and drain.
- Mix the sugar, salt, soy sauce, and chilli together, add to the shredded mango, mix thoroughly, and season additionally as desired. Then, add the mushroom and toss well. Place the salad on a bed of lettuce arranged on a platter and decorated with slices of shallot and spring onion.

(From p. 108)

- cut across into 1/2-cm thick slices, bean sprouts - remove the stringy ends of the roots and then immerse in boiling water for a few minutes, boiled egg - cut into 1/2-cm thick slices.
- Arrange a bed of lettuce on a platter and place the other ingredients on this. Pour on the salad dressing just before serving.

Yam Yai
Grand spicy Salad

Yam Het Nang Fa Het Fang lae Het Pao Heu
Spicy Mushrooms Salad

111

Yam Yai
Grand Spicy Salad

Ingredients
2 cakes firm white bean curd
3 cucumbers, 1 onion
1 large tomato, 2 lettuce plants
2 spring onions, 2 coriander plants
2-3 stalks celery
4-5 pickled garlic bulbs
1 small package mungbean noodles
200 grams roasted peanuts
2 limes, 1 cup mint leaves
2 chillies, 1 tsp. salt
1 tbsp. seasoning sauce
1 tbsp. palm sugar
1 tbsp. light soy sauce

Preparation
- Cut the cucumbers lengthwise into long, thin slices, or chop them.
- Cut the onion and tomato parallel to the core into thin slices.
- Cut the lettuce, spring onions, coriander, and celery into lengths.
- Slice the pickled garlic thin, and retain the brine. Pick the mint leaves from the stems. Cut the chillies lengthwise into very thin slices.
- Immerse the mungbean noodles in hot water until supple ; then, cut into lengths.
- Grind the peanuts fine. Fry the cakes of bean curd whole ; then, cut each in half, and cut each half into thin slices
- Place the cucumber in a mixing vessel, add the peanut and palm sugar, and blend while adding the soy sauce, seasoning sauce, lime juice, and pickled garlic brine. Add the bean curd, lettuce, onion, and tomato, and toss. Add the noodles and toss. The taste should be sour

(See p. 113)

Yam Het Nang Fa Het Fang lae Het Pao Heu
Spicy Mushrooms Salad

Ingredients
**100 grams each of ricestraw mushrooms, angel mushrooms, and abalone mushrooms
2 tbsp. shredded shallot
1 stalk celery
1 spring onion
1/2 cup mint leaves
1/2 tsp. chopped hot chilli
1/2 tsp. salt
1 tbsp. light soy sauce
3 tbsp. lime juice
1 tsp. sugar**

Preparation
- Wash the mushrooms, cutting off any foreign matter. Slice the ricestraw mushrooms in half. Cut off the tough portions from the bases of the angel and abalone mushrooms and then cut across into 1/4-inch strips.
- Arrange the mushrooms on a plate, place in a steamer in which the water is boiling, steam for a few minutes, remove from the steamer, and drain.
- Wash the celery and spring onion, cut off the roots and any dead or spoiled areas, and cut into 1/2-inch lengths.
- Mix the salt, sugar, soy sauce, and lime juice together, add to all the other ingredients, and toss well so the sauce penetrates the mushrooms. The taste should be sour, salty, and sweet.

(From p. 112)

and salty and also a little sweet. Add the celery, spring onion, coriander, and mint, toss, and transfer to a serving platter. Use chillies to decorate the salad. Coconut cream makes a delicious addition.

Yam Wun-sen
Mungbean Noodle in Spicy Salad

Yam Met Mamuang Himaphan
Spicy Fried Cashews

Yam Wun-sen
Mungbean Noodle in Spicy Salad

Ingredients

200 grams abalone mushrooms
200 grams ricestraw mushrooms
200 grams ear mushrooms, 300 grams mungbean noodles
20 fresh hot chillies
20 dried hot chillies, 200 grams spring onions
100 grams onions, 100 grams celery
3 tbsp. light soy sauce, 6-7 limes
100 grams palm sugar, 100 grams ripe tamarind
1 cake firm white bean curd, 100 grams garlic
100 grams shallots, 1 cup mint leaves

Preparation

- Immerse the mungbean noodles in boiling water to soften and then cut into convenient lengths.
- Tear the abalone mushrooms into shreds and immerse in boiling water a few minutes until done. Slice the ear mushrooms into thick pieces and immerse in boiling water until done. Cut the ricestraw mushrooms diagonally into thin slices, place in a frying pan without oil, sprinkle with salt, heat and stir and turn until done.
- Cut the spring onions and celery into sections. Peel the onions and cut into thin pieces lengthwise.
- Soak the tamarind in water for a time ; then, squeeze out the juice and mix this with the palm sugar and soy sauce. Heat to boiling and add additional soy sauce, sugar, or tamarind juice to obtain a sweet, salty, and sour taste.
- Mash the bean curd and cook in a frying pan without oil until pale yellow.
- Pound the fresh hot chillies and the garlic well in a mortar. Remove the seeds from the dried chillies, place in a dry frying pan together with the pounded fresh chillies and garlic, heat with regular turning until crisp, and then transfer to a mortar and pound fine.

(See p. 117)

Yam Met Mamuang Himaphan
Spicy Fried Cashews

Ingredients

300 grams cashews
2-3 spring onions
2-3 red spur chillies
1/2 tsp. salt
2 cups vegetable oil

Preparation

- Place the oil in a wok over medium heat. When the oil is hot, add the cashews and fry until golden ; then, remove them and drain.
- Wash the spring onions and chillies and allow to drain. Cut the spring onions into thin sections and cut the chillies across into thick slices.
- Toss the cashews with the spring onion, chilli, and salt, and serve.

(From p. 116)

- Toss together the mushrooms and mungbean noodles, adding the chilli mixture, tamarind sauce, and lime juice, and seasoning to taste. Add the onions, celery and spring onion. Dip the salad on a platter and garnish with mint leave.

Yam Thawai

Spicy Salad of Vegetables Blanched in Coconut Milk

118

Kaeng Liang
Spicy Vegetable Soup

Yam Thawai
Spicy Salad of Vegetables Blanched in Coconut Milk

Ingredients
1 bunch swamp cabbage
1 cup bean sprouts, hulls and root tips removed
1 bamboo shoot, 10 yard-long beans
1/2 banana blossom, 1 long eggplant
4 bell chillies, 3 tbsp. tamarind juice
1 tbsp. lime juice, 1 tbsp. light soy sauce, 2 tbsp. sugar
250 grams ricestraw mushrooms, caps expanded
500 grams grated coconut meat
2 tsp. turmeric powder
7 large dried chillies, soaked in water, seeds removed
4 shallots, 15 cloves garlic
1 stem lemon grass, 3 slices galangal
1 tsp. chopped coriander root
1/2 tsp. chopped kaffir lime rind
1 tsp. fermented bean paste

Preparation
- Mix the coconut with 2 cups of water, squeeze out 3 cups of coconut milk, and skim off 1 cup of coconut cream. Boil the mushrooms in the two remaining cups of coconut milk. When the mushrooms are done, remove them from the milk and set aside. Continue simmering the milk until the oil comes to the surface, transfer the milk to a pot, and set aside.

- In a mortar, pound the chillies, garlic, lemon grass, galangal, and kaffir lime rind until well ground. Add the 4 shallots and pound well. Add the fermented bean paste and mix in well. Now, add the boiled mushrooms and pound to grind and mix thoroughly.

- Transfer the spice mixture to a wok, add the coconut cream to the spices to disperse, and fry until fragrant. The taste should be very spicy, for this will be the dressing for the salad.

(See p. 121)

Kaeng Liang
Spicy Vegetable Soup

Ingredients
4 krachai roots, 50 grams shallots
300 grams ricestraw mushrooms
500 grams pumpkin, 1 tsp. pepper
1 tsp. fermented bean paste
1/2 cup sweet basil leaves (maeng lak)
2 cups gord gourd leaves
5 ears corn, 2 sponge gourds
2 tbsp. light soy sauce

Preparation
- Slice the kernels of corn from the cobs. Cut up the pumpkin and the gourds into chunks.
- Pound the pepper, krachai, shallots, and fermented bean paste together in a mortar enough to break and mix. The mixture need not be smooth. Add some water, stir, and then transfer to a pot and heat.
- Place the mushrooms in the mortar and pound a few strokes with the pestle to break them up. Add a little water, stir, and then add to the pot.
- When the pot comes to a boil, add the pumpkin and corn and cook until the pumpkin is tender. Add the gourd, and the gord gourd leaves and when it is just done, add the light soy sauce. Remove the pot from the heat, and add the basil leaves.

(From p. 120)

- Heat the pot of coconut milk. When it comes to a boil, cook the vegetables, one type at a time. When each kind is done, arrange it separately on a platter. When all the vegetables have been cooked, pour the dressing over them. Before serving, sprinkle with roasted sesame seed or fried thin slices of shallot.

Tom Phakkat Dong kap Mara
Bitter Gourd and Pickled Greens Soup

Kaeng Jeut Ruam Mit
Baby Corn, Mushroom, and Bean Curd Soup

THAI VEGETARIAN
FOOD

Tom Phakkat Dong kap Mara
Bitter Gourd and Pickled Greens Soup

Ingredients

1000 grams bitter gourd
1000 grams pickled mustard green
500 grams ricestraw mushrooms
5 cakes firm white bean curd
2 garlic bulbs
1 tbsp. pepper
7 coriander roots
1 tbsp. salt
1 tbsp. palm sugar
3 tbsp. fermented soybeans
2 tbsp. dark soy sauce
2 tbsp. light soy sauce
vegetable oil

Preparation

- Clean and wash the mushrooms and cut in half lengthwise.
- Wash the mustard green and cut into bite-sized pieces.
- Cut the bitter gourds up into large pieces and then fry in oil. When they are done, set aside.
- Wash the bean curd and cut into bite-sized chunks. Fry in oil until browned and then drain.
- Pound the coriander roots, garlic, and pepper in a mortar until thoroughly ground. Heat 3 tbsp. of oil in a frying pan. When hot, fry the garlic mixture until it yellows ; then, add the dark soy sauce, fermented soybeans, palm sugar, and salt and fry with turning and stirring until fragrant. Add the pickled mustard green, bean curd, mushrooms, bitter gourds and enough clean water to almost cover the mixture. Season with light soy sauce. Simmer over low heat for 30 minutes.

Kaeng Jeut Ruam Mit
Baby Corn, Mushroom, and Bean Curd Soup

Ingredients

4 cups vegetable stock (See p.64)
100 grams ricestraw mushrooms
2 cakes soft white bean curd
100 grams baby corn
100 grams squash cut into 1/2-inch squares
1 tbsp. light soy sauce
1/2 tsp. salt
1/2 tsp. sugar
2 spring onions
1 tbsp. fried garlic
1/4 tsp. ground pepper
1 coriander green, chopped coarsely

Preparation

- Wash the mushrooms and the baby corn. Cut the corn into short lengths. Slice the bean curd into cubes.
- In a pot, bring the stock to a boil, add the squash, and cook until tender. Then, add the baby corn, bean curd, and mushrooms.
- Season with salt, soy sauce, sugar, and pepper.
- Cut the spring onions into short lengths, add to the soup, stir, and remove from the heat. Sprinkle with chopped coriander greens before serving.

Jap Chai
Vegetable Potpourri

Mara Yat Sai
Stuffed Bitter Gourds in Mushroom Broth

127

Jap Chai
Vegetable Potpourri

Ingredients
**300 grams cabbage
300 grams Chinese kale
300 grams celery
200 grams garlic plants
300 grams Chinese mustard green
300 grams Chinese radish
300 grams mushrooms with expanded caps
3-4 coriander roots
4-5 bulbs garlic
2-3 cake firm white bean curd, each cut into
four triangular pieces and fried
1 tbsp. palm sugar
2 tsp. salt
2 tbsp. light soy sauce
2 tbsp. vegetable oil
1 tbsp. seasoning sauce
1 tbsp. dark soy sauce**

Preparation
- Cut the head of cabbage into eight sections. Cut all the other vegetables into large pieces.
- Pound the garlic and coriander root together in a mortar, place in the hot oil in the frying pan, and fry a few moments until fragrant.
- Add all of the vegetables and mix with the spatula. Add some water and salt, light soy sauce, palm sugar, and seasoning sauce. When satisfied with the taste, transfer the mixture to the pot, add the mushrooms and fried bean curd and dark soy sauce, and then simmer slowly until the vegetables are tender.

Mara Yat Sai
Stuffed Bitter Gourds in Mushroom Broth

Ingredients

3 Chinese bitter gourds
200 grams ricestraw mushrooms
200 grams wheat gluten
1/2 tbsp. peeled garlic cloves
1/2 tsp. pepper
2 tbsp.light soy sauce
3 cups water

Preparation

- Clean and wash the mushrooms, boil until done, and then chop fine in a blender. Save the water in which the mushrooms were boiled.
- Cut the bitter gourds in half and remove the insides.
- Pound the garlic well and then mix with the wheat gluten. Add the pepper and light soy sauce and then the chopped mushrooms and mix until stiff. Stuff the bitter gourds with this mixture.
- Place the stuffed gourds in a steamer in which the water is boiling and steam for about ten minutes.
- Heat the mushrooms stock to boiling, add the stuffed gourds, and season with light soy sauce.

Satu
Stew

Tom Yam Kathi kap Kalampli
Sour and Spicy Cabbage and Coconut Cream Soup

Satu
Stew

Ingredients
1 sweet potato
2 carrots, 2 onions
300 grams ricestraw mushrooms
20 cherry tomatoes
200 grams green beans
3 cakes firm white bean curd
1 tsp. salt, 1/2 tsp. pepper
1 cup vegetable oil
1 tbsp. light soy sauce
1 tbsp. dark soy sauce
2 1/2 cups vegetable stock (See p. 61)
2 tbsp. arrowroot starch
1 tbsp catsup

Preparation
- Wash and peel the potato, cut into large cubes, and fry in the oil.
- Peel the carrots and cut into 1-inch sections. Peel the onions and cut into quarters if small or into sixths if large.
- Clean the mushrooms and cut into halves lengthwise.
- Cut off the ends of the green beans, slice into 1 1/2-inch sections.
- Cut the bean curd into triangular pieces about 1/2-inch thick and marinate in the dark soy sauce.
- Heat about 10 tbsp. of oil in a frying pan. When the oil is hot, fry the marinated bean curd. When the curd has become brown and firm, add the mushrooms, then the stock, and then season with catsup, salt, light soy sauce, and pepper. Add the potato, carrots, onions, tomatoes and green beans.
- Mix the arrowroot starch with water, and add to the stew when it has almost reached the boiling point. Stir and see if the stew is thick enough ; if not, add a little more of the starch and water mixture.
- After the stew has come to a boil, remove from the heat.

Tom Yam Kathi kap Kalampli
Sour and Spicy Cabbage and
Coconut Cream Soup

Ingredients
500 grams grated coconut meat
500 grams cabbage
5 roasted shallots
2 dried large chillies, roasted and well pounded
1 large garlic bulb
1 lemongrass cut into short lengths
2-3 kaffir lime leaves, torn into halves
2-3 sliced galangal
3-4 tbsp. lime juice
3-4 tbsp. light soy sauce
1 tbsp. fried sliced shallot

Preparation
- Mix 3 cups of warm water with the coconut and squeeze out 4 cups of coconut milk.
- Remove the outermost layer of leaves from the cabbage. Discard the outer leaves, wash the head, cut into 2-inch squares. Remove the hard core and discard.
- Pound the shallots and garlic well in a mortar, add the ground chilli, and pound to mix thoroughly.
- Place the coconut milk in a pot over medium heat and, stirring constantly, bring to a boil. Add the lemon grass, kaffir lime leaves and galangal. Add the cabbage and when it is done, mix the lime juice and soy sauce into the spice mixture and add to the pot, seasoning further if necessary. Before serving, sprinkle with fried shallot.

Tom Yam Het
Sour and Spicy Mushroom Soup

Tao-hu Luk Khoei
Fried Bean Curd in Savory Syrup

Tom Yam Het
Sour and Spicy Mushroom Soup

Ingredients
500 grams ricestraw mushrooms
3 cups water
1 lemon grass stem cut into sections
2-3 slices of galangal
3 kaffir lime leaves
3 tbsp. light soy sauce
3 tbsp. lime juice
10 hot chillies, either fresh, or dried and fried crisp
1 chopped spring onion or coriander plant

Preparation
- Clean the mushroom by slicing off any dark areas and debris and wash well. If the mushrooms are large, cut them in half.
- Bring the water to a boil, add the galangal, lemon grass torn kaffir lime leaves, and the mushrooms. When the mushrooms are just tender, add the soy sauce and remove from the heat. Add the lime juice to obtain a sour and salty taste. Add the crisp fried dried chillies or crushed fresh chillies, sprinkle with chopped spring onion or coriander, and serve hot.

Tao-hu Luk Khoei
Fried Bean Curd in Savory Syrup

Ingredients

3 cakes firm white bean curd
3 tbsp. vegetable oil
3 shallots, sliced
10 cloves garlic, sliced
1 small dried spur chilli, sliced
1/4 cup palm sugar
1/4 cup tamarind juice
1/4 cup light soy sauce
1 coriander plant

Preparation

- Wash the bean curd and cut each cake into quarters.
- Fry separately the shallot, the garlic, and the chilli until each is crisp ; then, set aside.
- Fry the bean curd in the oil in which the shallot was fried. When beginning to brown, remove from the pan.
- Return the pan to the heat and to the remaining oil add the sugar, tamarind juice, and soy sauce. Cook with regular stirring until thick.
- Just before serving, place the fried bean curd on a plate, pour the syrup over it, and sprinkle with the fried garlic, shallot, and chilli and with fresh coriander leaves.

Tao-hu Neung Song Khreuang
Steamed Bean Curd in Sauce

Tun Het Hawm Sai Sa-rai Sen Phom
Shiitake Mushroom and Sea Moss Stew

Tao-hu Neung Song Khreuang
Steamed Bean Curd in Sauce

Ingredients

3 tubes soft bean curd
1 tbsp. minced ginger
3 tbsp. fermented soybean
1 tbsp. sugar
1/2 tbsp. light soy sauce
3-4 coriander roots
5 peeled garlic cloves
5 pepper corns
2 tbsp. vegetable oil
1 tbsp. coriander leaves

Preparation

- Cut the bean curd into discs about one inch thick.
- Pound the ginger, garlic, pepper, and coriander roots in a mortar. They need not be finely ground.
- Heat the oil in a wok. When hot, add the fermented soybean and the ground ginger-garlic mixture and stir fry over low heat until fragrant. Add the sugar and soy sauce and continue cooking. When thickened, remove from the heat.
- Place the bean curd discs on a plate, pour the fried spices over them, and then place the plate in a steamer in which the water is boiling. Steam about 10 minutes, remove from the steamer, sprinkle with coriander leaf, and serve.

Tun Het Hawm Sai Sa-rai Sen Phom
Shiitake Mushroom and Sea Moss Stew

Ingredients
8-10 shiitake mushrooms
25 grams sea moss
2 tbsp. light soy sauce
1/4 tsp. salt
1/4 tsp. sugar
10 pepper corns, broken
1 tbsp. vegetable oil
1 tsp. crushed garlic

Preparation
- Wash the mushrooms and then soak in water until softened. If the mushrooms are large, slice into bite-sized pieces. Retain the water in which the mushrooms were soaked. Heat the oil in a wok. When hot, add the garlic and mushrooms and fry until fragrant ; then remove from the wok.
- Wash the sea moss and then soak until softened ; then, remove from the water and set aside.
- Place the water in which the mushrooms were soaked in a pot, add the mushrooms, sea moss, soy sauce, salt, sugar and pepper, simmer until tender (about 10-15 minutes), and then serve.

Lap Het kap Tao-hu Khaeng
Spicy Chopped Mushroom and Bean Curd

Nam Phrik Makham
Green Tamarind Chilli Paste

Lap Het kap Tao-hu Khaeng
Spicy Chopped Mushroom and Bean Curd

Ingredients
300 grams ricestraw mushrooms
100 grams ear mushrooms
1 cake firm white bean curd
1 tsp. ground dried hot chilli
2 tbsp. ground parched rice
3 shallots
3 slices young galangal
2 limes
7 stems mint
4 spring onions
1 phak chi farang plant
3 tbsp. light soy sauce

Preparation

- Cut the mushrooms into thin slices, boil for a few minutes, remove, from water, and allow to cool.
- Mash the bean curd fine and heat in a wok fry and turn to dry.
- Heat the galangal in a wok until golden and then pound fine in a mortar.
- Cut the shallots parallel to the core into thin slices. Squeeze the limes, collecting the juce in a bowl.
- Chop the phak chi farang plant and spring onion coarsely. Pick the mint leaves from the stems.
- Toss the mushrooms and bean curd with the parched rice, ground chilli, galangal, shallot, soy sauce, and lime juice. Season additionally as desired. Add the mint leaves, spring onion, and phak chi farang. Serve with fresh vegetables.

Nam Phrik Makham
Green Tamarind Chilli Paste

Ingredients

200 grams green tamarinds
5 tbsp. fermented bean paste
100 grams palm sugar
8 hot chillies
3 tbsp. light soy sauce
8 cloves. garlic
2 tbsp. vegetable oil

Preparation

- Pound the garlic and tamarinds to a paste and then mix in the fermented bean paste. Then, add the chillies and break them open with a few strokes with the pestle.
- Heat the oil in a frying pan. When it is hot, add the paste and fry with regular turning and stirring.
- Add the soy sauce and palm sugar and continue frying until the mixture dries, adding palm sugar or soy sauce to suit your taste.

Nam Phrik Ong
Northern Style Chilli Paste

146

Nam Phrik Phao Thuao Khiao
Spicy Mungbean Sauce

Nam Phrik Ong
Northern Style Chilli Paste

Ingredients

5 cakes firm white bean curd
300 grams shallots, 100 grams garlic
200 grams cherry tomatoes
10 dried large chillies
200 grams ricestraw mushrooms
1/4 cup vegetable oil, 1 tbsp. light soy sauce
1 tsp. salt, 3 tbsp. tamarind juice

Preparation

- Mash the bean curd well.
- Pound the garlic thoroughly in a mortar. Cut the shallots into thin slices.
- Wash the mushrooms and chop finely.
- Soak the chillies in water to soften ; then, remove the seeds and pound the skins well in a mortar.
- Soak the ripe tamarind in water.
- Heat a good volume of oil vigorously in a frying pan. Add portions of the mashed bean curd and fry so that they puff up. The portions of curd should remain together as fluffy cakes when frying. When crisp on the outside still tender inside, remove the curd from the oil and arrow to drain.
- In a frying pan with a small amount of oil, fry the shallot, garlic, and chilli, with regular stirring and turning. Add the fried bean curd, stirring and breaking up the cakes with a spatula. Season to taste with soy sauce, and salt.
- Add the mushrooms and tamarind juice and mix in by turning with the spatula. If the mixture in dry, add a little water.
- Cut the tomatoes in half and add to the pan. The taste should be sour, salty, and hot. Season further as necessary ; if you would like to sweeten the chilli

(See p. 149)

Nam Phrik Phao Thua Khiao
Spicy Mungbean Sauce

Ingredients
3/4 cup finely ground steamed hulled mungbeans
3/4 cup crisp-fried, air-dried slices of shallot
1/2 cup crisp-fried, air-dried slices of garlic
10-15 freshly dried large chillies
1/3 cup palm sugar
1/3 cup light soy sauce
1/4 cup tamarind juice
1/4 cup vegetable oil

Preparation
- Remove the seeds from the chillies and cut across into thin slices. Heat some oil in a wok. When hot, add the chillies and remove the wok from the heat. Stir the chillies in the oil long enough so that they will be crisp when cool ; then, remove them from the oil. Be cautious in frying the chillies, for if overcooked, they become bitter.
- Pound separately in a mortar the onion, the garlic, and the chilli, until fine ; then, mix together.
- Heat the 1/4 cup of oil in a wok over low heat. When hot, add the chilli-garlic-onion mixture and fry with stirring and turning. When well mixed, add the sugar, soy sauce, and tamarind juice ; then, add the mungbean and mix well. When the mixture comes to a boil, taste to see whether the flavor is spicy hot, salty, sweet, and sour, and season as necessary. Do not allow to become too thick when frying, for as it cools, the chilli paste becomes thicker. When the chilli paste has cooled, store in a clean,dry jar. Serve with rice or spread on bread.

(From p. 148)

paste, add some palm sugar.
- Serve with fresh, steamed, or boiled vegetables.

THAI VEGETARIAN
FOOD

Tao-jiao Lon
Fermented Soybeans in Coconut Cream

150

Kaeng Som Taeng-mo On
Spicy Sour Green Watermelon Soup

Tao-jiao Lon
Fermented Soybeans in Coconut Cream

Ingredients
300 grams light fermented soybeans
500 grams grated coconut meat
10 shallots
300 grams ricestraw mushrooms
3 tbsp. tamarind juice
200 grams palm sugar
6 red, and yellow chillies

Preparation
- Add 1/2 cup water to the coconut and squeeze to obtain 1 cup of thick coconut cream.
- Slice the shallots and mushroom into large pieces.
- Place the fermented soybeans in a collander and wash until the salty taste is gone. Pound the soybeans in a mortar and then mix with the coconut cream. Alternatively, the beans may be placed in a blender with the coconut cream. In either case, the soybeans should be neither too fine nor too coarse in texture.
- Place the soybeans and coconut cream in a pot and add the mushrooms. Heat the pot and add the palm sugar and tamarind juice, stirring constantly. Then, add the shallot. The taste should be salty and sweet and also sour. Add red and yellow chillies for color.
- Serve with cucumbers, yard-long beans, krathin, cabbage, banana blossom, winged beans, carrot and ma kheua proa.

Kaeng Som Taeng-mo On
Spicy Sour Green Watermelon Soup

Ingredients

1000 grams small, green watermelon
500 grams ricestraw mushrooms
3 tbsp. tamarind juice
1 tbsp. palm sugar
2 tbsp. light soy sauce
1 tsp. salt
4 cups water

Spice mixture
10 cloves garlic
7 shallots
10 dried large chillies
1 tsp. fermented bean paste

Preparation

- Pound the spice mixture ingredients in a mortar until thoroughly ground and mixed.
- Place the spice mixture in a pot containing water and stir to disperse. Heat and add the mushrooms, tamarind juice, palm sugar, soy sauce, and salt to taste. When the flavor is right, add the watermelon.
- When the soup comes to a boil, remove from the heat and serve.

Kaeng Khiao Wan Tao-hu
Bean Curd Green Curry

Kaeng Khua Sapparot
Pineapple Curry

Kaeng Khiao Wan Tao-hu
Bean Curd Green Curry

Ingredients
4 cakes firm white bean curd
300 grams grated coconut meat
100 grams ma-kheua phuang
100 grams boiled bamboo shoot
2-3 tbsp. light soy sauce, 1 tbsp. palm sugar
2 stems sweet basil (horapha)
2 kaffir lime leaves

Spice Mixture
20 hot chillies, 10 green chillies
5 shallots, 10 large cloves garlic
1 tsp. thinly sliced galangal
1 tbsp. thinly sliced lemon grass
1/2 tsp. thinly sliced kaffir lime rind
1 tsp. chopped coriander root, 5 pepper corns
1 tsp. ground roasted coriander seeds
1 tsp. ground roasted cumin, 1 tsp. salt

Preparation

- Pound the spice mixture ingredients together in a mortar until thoroughly ground and mixed.
- Slice the bean curd into one-half-inch cubes.
- Mix 1 1/2 cups warm water with the grated coconut and squeeze out 2 1/2 cups coconut milk.
- Remove the stems from the ma-kheua phuang. Slice the bamboo shoot into lengths about 1/2 inch thick.
- Pick the sweet basil leaves from the stem, which is discarded. Tear the kaffir lime leaves.
- Skim 1 cup of coconut cream from the coconut milk. In a frying pan, heat the cream until the oil surfaces, add the spice mixture, and stir until well dispersed and fragrant. Add the bean curd and continue stirring lightly.
- Transfer to a pot, add the remaining coconut milk, and bring to a boil. Add the ma-kheua phuang, and bamboo shoot, and light soy sauce and palm sugar to taste. Add the sweet basil and kaffir lime leaves and remove from heat.

Kaeng Khua Sapparot
Pineapple Curry

Ingredients

1 pineapple
500 grams ricestraw mushrooms
1000 grams grated coconut meat
1 cup soybeans
3 cakes firm white bean curd
1/4 cup vegetable oil
1 tbsp. palm sugar
2 tbsp. light soy sauce

Spice Mixture

6 slices galangal
6 lemon grass, finely sliced
50 grams shallots
50 grams garlic
20 dried hot chillies
1/2 tbsp. finely sliced kaffir lime rind
2-3 coriander roots, chopped
1 tsp. fermented bean paste

Preparation

- Peel the pineapple, remove the eyes, and chop into small pieces. Wash and clean the mushrooms and cut into pieces.
- Add 3 cups of warm water to the coconut and squeeze out 4 cups of coconut milk. Skim 1 cup of coconut cream from the milk, heat coconut milk to boiling, and then remove from the heat.
- Place the spice mixture ingredients in a mortar and pound until thoroughly ground and mixed.
- Fry the spice mixture ingredients in oil until fragrant, add the mushrooms, and then the soybeans and bean curd, stirring and turning to mix well.
- Transfer the contents of the frying pan to the pot of coconut milk and bring to a boil, add the pineapple, and season to taste with sugar and soy sauce. Add the coconut cream just before removing from the heat.

Kaeng Matsaman
Massaman Curry

Kaeng Kari Tao-hu Leuang
Savory Bean Curd Curry

Kaeng Matsaman
Massaman Curry

Ingredients
500 grams ricestraw or abalone mushrooms
300 grams wheat gluten
4 cakes firm white bean curd
1000 grams grated coconut meat
300 grams roasted peanuts, 500 grams onions
4 potatoes or sweet potatoes
1 small pumpkin, 1 pineapple
4 tbsp. tamarind juice, 3 tbsp. light soy sauce, 2 tbsp. citron juice
1/4 cup vegetable oil, 2 tbsp. palm sugar

Spice Mixture
7 red chillies, 1/2 cup thinly sliced shallots
1/2 cup thinly sliced garlic, 1 tsp. thinly sliced galangal
1 tbsp. thinly sliced lemon grass
1 tbsp. coriander seeds, 3 cardamoms
3 cloves, 1 tbsp. cumin, 1/2 tsp. nutmeg, 1 tsp. mace
1/2 tsp. cinnamon, 1 tbsp. salt

Preparation
- In a dry frying pan, parch all the spice mixture ingredients over low heat until fragrant ; then, transfer them to a mortar and pound until thoroughly ground and mixed.
- Slice the mushrooms into large pieces.
- Cut the bean curd into squares, fry until golden, and drain.
- Form the raw wheat gluten into thin patties, fry until golden brown, and cut into large pieces.
- Cut the pumpkin, pineapple, potato, and onions into large pieces.
- Add 4 cups of water to the coconut and squeeze the grated coconut to obtain 6 cups of coconut milk. Skim 1 cup of coconut cream from the milk.
- Heat the coconut cream in a frying pan until the oil surfaces ; then, add the spice mixture and stir continuously until well-dispersed and fragrant. Transfer to a pot over medium heat, add the remaining coconut cream, the bean curd, mushrooms, fried wheat gluten,

(See p. 161)

Kaeng Kari Tao-hu Leuang
Savory Bean Curd Curry

Ingredients
3 cakes firm yellow bean curd
500 grams grated coconut meat
2 tbsp. fried sliced shallot
3 potatoes, 2 tsp. salt.

Spice Mixture
3 large dried chillies, seeds removed
1 tsp. salt, 1 tbsp. finely sliced lemon grass
5 broiled shallots, 1 broiled garlic bulb
1 tbsp. finely sliced broiled ginger
1 tsp. finely sliced broiled galangal
1 tbsp. ground pan-roasted coriander seed
1 tsp. ground pan-roasted cumin seed
2 tsp. curry powder

Preparation
- Cut each cake of bean curd into six pieces.
- Add 2 cups of warm water to the coconut and squeeze out 3 cups of coconut milk. Skim 1 cup of coconut cream from the milk.
- Pound the spice mixture ingredients in a mortar until ground and mixed thoroughly. Fry in the oil used for frying the shallot until fragrant ; then, add the coconut cream and continue frying until fragrant.
- Add the bean curd, fry, and then dip the mixture into a pot, add the coconut milk, season to obtain a salty taste, and place on heat to simmer. Peel and quarter the potatoes and add to the pot. When the curry has thickened a little, remove from the heat. It may be necessary to add some more salt.
- When ready to serve, sprinkle with fried shallot and serve with pickled cucumbers, pickled ginger, or a spicy salad.

(From p. 160)

peanuts, pumpkin, onions, pineapple, and potato.
- Season to taste with citron juice, tamarind juice, palm sugar, and light soy sauce. When the potatoes are done, remove from heat.

Kaeng Phet Tao-hu Khao Het Thua Lantao
Red Curry of Bean Curd, Mushroom and Peas

Kaeng Hang Le Tao-hu Sai Sapparot
Bean Curd and Pineapple in Northern-Style Curry

Kaeng Phet Tao-hu Khao Het Thua Lantao

Red Curry of Bean Curd, Mushrooms and Peas

Ingredients

300 grams ricestraw mushrooms, caps still in their sheaths
2 cakes firm white bean curd
200 grams peas
400 grams grated coconut
2-3 kaffir lime leaves
2 stems sweet basil (horapha)
3 tbsp. light soy sauce

Spice Mixture

3 dried spur chillies
5 shallots, 2 garlic bulbs
1/2 tsp. thinly sliced galangal
1 heaping tbsp. thinly sliced lemon grass
1 tsp. thinly sliced kaffir lime rind
2 tsp. thinly sliced coriander root
5 pepper corns, 1 tsp. salt
2 tsp. coriander seeds, 1/2 tsp. cumin

Preparation

- Thoroughly pound all the spice mixture ingredients in a mortar.
- Wash and clean the mushrooms. If they are large, slice in half.
- Wash the bean curd, pat dry, and cut into 1/2-inch squares.
- Wash the peas and set aside to drain.
- Mix the coconut with 1 cup warm water and squeeze out 2 cups of coconut milk.
- Skim 1/2 cup coconut cream from the coconut milk. Heat the cream in a frying pan until the oil surfaces and then add the spice mixture and cook with stirring and turning until fragrant. Add the bean curd and the peas, cook for a few moments, then transfer the contents of the pan to a pot. Add the remaining coconut milk, heat to boiling, and add the mushrooms. When the mushrooms are done, pluck the sweet basil leaves from the stems and add to the pot. Tear the kaffir lime leaves and add. Season to taste with soy sauce, stir well, and remove from the heat.

Kaeng Hang Le Tao-hu Sai Sapparot
Bean Curd and Pineapple in Northern-Style Curry

Ingredients

3 cakes firm white bean curd
1 small pineapple
1/4 cup thinly sliced young ginger
20 peeled cloves of garlic
2 cups water
3 four-inch long pods ripe tamarind soaked in 1/4 cup water
1 tbsp. palm sugar

Spice Mixture

3 dried spur chillies
5 peeled cloves of garlic
5 peeled shallots
2 tsp. salt
1 tbsp. finely sliced lemon grass
2 tsp. curry powder
1 tbsp. light fermented soybeans

Preparation

- In a mortar, pound the chillies, salt, and lemon grass. Add the garlic and shallots and pound together. Then, add the fermented soybeans, and curry powder, and pound to mix thoroughly.
- Wash the bean curd and cut each cake into quarters. Peel the pineapple, remove the eyes, cut into quarters, remove core, and slice each quarter into two-inch pieces.
- Toss the pieces of bean curd with the spice mixture, place in a pot, add the water, and put on a low heat. Add the pineapple, ginger, and garlic and simmer slowly until the pineapple becomes tender. Season with the sugar, tamarind juice, and salt to obtain a sour, salty, and spicy hot taste.

Phanaeng Het kap Tao-hu
Bean Curd in Thick Curry

Kaeng Khi Lek
A Rich Tradditional Thai Curry

Phanaeng Het kap Tao-hu
Bean Curd in Thick Curry

Ingredients
200 grams large ricestraw mushrooms
3 cakes firm white bean curd
250 grams grated coconut meat
1 tbsp. light soy sauce
2 shredded kaffir lime leaves
1 shredded red spur chilli
1 tbsp. palm sugar
1 tbsp. vegetable oil for stir frying
1 cup vegetable oil for deep frying

Spice Mixture
5 large dried chillies
5 shallots
10 cloves garlic
1 tsp. fine slices of galangal
1 tsp. thin slices of lemon grass
1/2 tbsp. finely sliced kaffir lime rind
1 tsp. finely chopped coriander root
5 pepper corns
1 tsp. salt

Preparation
- Pound the spice mixture ingredients in a mortar until ground and mixed thoroughly.
- Add 1/2 cup water to the grated coconut and squeeze out 1 cup of coconut cream.
- Cut the bean curd into thick slices. Heat one cup of oil in a wok. When hot, fry the bean curd until golden ; then, remove and drain.
- Slice the mushrooms in half, scald in boiling water, and drain.
- Heat 1 tbsp. oil in a wok and then fry the spice mixture until fragrant. Add the coconut cream and continue frying until the oil surfaces. Add the soy sauce and palm sugar and mix ; then, add the bean curd and then the mushrooms.
- Dip into a serving dish, sprinkle with kaffir lime leaves and spur chilli.

Kaeng Khi Lek
A Rich Traditional Thai Curry

Ingredients
500 grams boiled khi lek leaves and blossoms
500 grams grated coconut meat
3 sheets yuba
250 grams abalone mushrooms
1 bunch ya-nang leaves
salt, palm sugar, light soy sauce

Spice Mixture
3 large dried Bang Chang chillies
3 slices galangal
1 lemon grass stem
3 bulbs garlic, 3 shallots
5 kra-chai roots
1 cake fermented bean curd

Preparation
- Squeeze the coconut to obtain 2 cups of coconut milk. Separate the cream from the milk.
- Crush and squeeze the ya-nang leaves in 3 cups of water.
- Cut the yuba into pieces and soak in water.
- Roast the abalone mushroom and then tear or slice into pieces.
- Wrap the fermented bean curd in banana leaf and roast until dried.
- Pound the spice mixture ingredients, including the roasted bean curd, in a mortar until thoroughly ground and mixed.
- Heat some of the coconut cream in a wok until the oil surfaces ; then, add the spices mixture, stir to disperse, and fry until fragrant.
- Then, add the khi lek leaves and blossoms, the yuba, and mushroom, and mix well. Add the coconut milk and the water in which the ya-nang leaves were squeezed. Season to taste with salt, palm sugar, and soy sauce. Simmer for a short while and then add remaining coconut cream. Allow to return to a boil and then remove from the heat.

Ho Mok
Mushrooms Steamed in Spiced Coconut Sauce

Ngop Khao Phot
Roasted Corn in Spicy Coconut Sauce

Ho Mok
Mushrooms Steamed in Spiced Coconut Sauce

Ingredients
300 grams ricestraw mushrooms or abalone mushrooms
500 grams grated coconut meat
3 tbsp. ground roasted peanuts, 1-2 tbsp. wheat flour
2 tbsp. uncooked rice soaked in water
sweet basil (horapha) leaves, yo leaves, Chinese cabbage
kaffir lime leaves, coriander
red spur chillies, light soy sauce

Spice Mixture
3 dried large chillies, 5 shallots, 3 garlic bulbs
1 stem lemon grass, 1 slice galangal
5 coriander roots, 2 krachai roots, 10 hot chillies, 1 tsp. salt

Preparation
● Remove the sweet basil leaves from the stems, wash the leaves well, and drain. Wash the Chinese cabbage, slice into pieces, scald, and drain. Wash the mushrooms well and cut diagonally into thin slices.

● Remove the soaked rice from the water, pound until finely ground in a mortar, and set aside.

● Place all the spice mixture ingredients in mortar and pound to a fine-textured paste ; the mix in the ground soaked rice.

● Place the coconut in cheesecloth, add some water, squeeze out 1/2 cup of coconut cream, set this aside, and then squeeze the coconut again to obtain about one more cup of coconut milk.

● Place the coconut milk in a large bowl with the spice mixture and blend together, adding the mushrooms and the soy sauce. Sprinkle a little flour on the mass in the bowl, mix in well, add a little more flour and mix, and continue in this way until the mixture is thick.

● Line the bottoms of banana leaf or porcelain cups with yo leaves, sweet basil leaves, and/or Chinese cabbage leaves and then fill the cups with the mixture. Top with a little of the coconut cream.

(See p. 173)

Ngop Khao Phot
Roasted Corn in Spicy Coconut Sauce

Ingredients

**5 ears tender corn, 1 bunch holy basil
200 grams shredded coconut meat
200 grams grated coconut meat
2 tbsp. light soy sauce, 1 tbsp. palm sugar**

Spice Mixture
2 large lemon grass stems
75 grams galangal, 50 grams krachai
1 tbsp. salt, 1 tbsp. turmeric, 2 cakes fermented bean paste
1 tsp. shredded kaffir lime rind

Preparation

- Slice up the lemon grass galangal, krachai and turmeric and pound in a mortar with the salt and kaffir lime rind until thoroughly ground and mixed.
- Roast the fermented bean paste cakes until fragrant, add to the mortar, and pound to grind and mix with the other ingredients. Next, add the shredded coconut and pound to mix thoroughly.
- Slice the kernels of corn from the cob and mix with the other ingredients, adding the palm sugar, holy basil leaves, and soy sauce.
- Mix some water to the grated coconut and squeeze to obtain a thick coconut cream, and mix this thoroughly with the other ingredients. Roll this mixture in two or three layers of banana leaf, and pin the wrappers closed with toothpicks or slivers of wood.
- Roast over a very low fire. If the fire is too hot, the leaves will burn through before the corn is cooked.

(From p. 172)

- Cut the kaffir lime leaves into fine strips and the chilli into thin slices, sprinkle these on the surface of the mixture in each cup. Place the cups in the tray of a steamer and steam over medium heat.

Priao Wan Mangsawirat
Sweet and Sour Stir-Fried Vegetable

Het Hu Nu Phat Khai
Ear Mushroom Stir-Fried in Egg

175

Priao Wan Mangsawirat
Sweet and Sour Stir-Fried Vegetable

Ingredients

3 cucumbers
1 onion
1/4 pineapple
2 large tomatoes
1 cake firm white bean curd, cut into eighths
3 tbsp. vegetable oil
1 tsp. sugar
1 tbsp. light soy sauce
1 tsp. salt
3 cloves garlic, crushed and chopped

Preparation

- Wash the cucumbers, peel if you like, cut lengthwise into quarters, and cut each quarter in half. Peel the onion, cut off the two ends, cut top to bottom in half, and then cut each half into wedges 1/4 inch thick at the thickest side. If you wish, use a sweet pepper in this dish, seeds removed and cut up in the same way as the onion.

- Peel and eye the pineapple, remove the hard core, and cut into 1-inch pieces.

- Fry the garlic until fragrant, add the bean curd, and fry with regular turning until golden. Add the onion. When tender, add the pineapple and then the cucumber.

- Cut the tomatoes into wedges 1/2 inch thick at the thickest, and add to the pan. Add the salt, sugar, and soy sauce and cook with turning and stirring until the vegetables are done ; then, dip onto a platter and serve hot.

Het Hu Nu Phat Khai
Ear Mushroom Stir-Fried in Egg

Ingredients

300 grams ear mushrooms
1 egg, beaten
3 spring onions
3 red spur chillies
1 tbsp. chopped garlic
2 tbsp. vegetable oil
1 tbsp. light soy sauce

Preparation

- Wash the mushrooms, remove the bases, and cut into bite-sized pieces.
- Cut the spring onions into two-inch lengths. Slice the spur chillies diagonally.
- Heat the oil in a wok. When hot, add the garlic and fry until golden ; then, add the mushrooms and spur chilli and fry with stirring and turning. Season to taste with the soy sauce and stir well. Pour the egg into the wok and fry, scraping and turning with the spatula. When the egg has set, add the spring onion, stir the mixture well, and then dip onto a serving platter.

Het Nang Fa Phat Tao-hu
Stir-Fried Angel Mushrooms and Bean Curd

Phat Thua Fak Yao Sai Khai
Stir-Fried Yard Long Beans with Egg

Het Nang Fa Phat Tao-hu
Stir-Fried Angel Mushrooms and Bean Curd

Ingredients
300 grams angel mushrooms
1 cake semi-firm yellow bean curd
2 spring onions
1 tbsp. chopped garlic
1/4 tsp. pepper
1 tbsp. light soy sauce
1/2 cup vegetable oil

Preparation
- Wash the mushrooms and cut into bite-sized pieces.
- Cut the bean curd into quarters.
- Wash the spring onions and cut into lengths.
- Heat the oil in a wok. Fry the bean curd over medium heat until golden on both sides ; then, move the bean curd to one side, remove all but about 2 tablespoonsful of the oil, add the garlic and fry over low heat until fragrant.
- Turn the heat to high, add the mushrooms, move the bean curd to the center of the wok, add the soy sauce, pepper, and spring onion, stir and turn the mixture two or three times, and then remove from the heat and serve.

Phat Thua Fak Yao Sai Khai
Stir-Fried Yard-Long Beans with Egg

Ingredients
**300 grams yard-long beans
5 cloves garlic, chopped
3 tbsp. vegetable oil
2 eggs, beaten
2 tbsp. light soy sauce
2 tbsp. water**

Preparation
- Wash the beans and cut into 1-inch lengths.
- Fry the garlic in the oil until yellowed, add the beans, soy sauce, and water, and cook with the pan covered until the beans are done.
- Pour the beaten eggs into the pan and stir to mix the egg and the beans. When the egg is done, dip onto a plate and serve.

Khao Phot On kap Tho-hu Phat Phrik Sot
Spicy Stir-Fried Baby Corn and Bean Curd

Tao-hu Thot Song Khreuang
Fried Bean Curd and Vegetables in Sauce

Khao Phot On kap
Tao-hu Phat Phrik Sot
Spicy Stir-Fried Baby Corn and Bean Curd

Ingredients
2 cakes firm yellow bean curd
10 ears baby corn
1 tbsp. chopped garlic
1 tbsp. light soy sauce
1/2 tsp. salt
1/2 tbsp. seasoning sauce
1/2 tsp. sugar
5 spur chillies
1/4 cup vegetable oil
sweet basil (horapha) leaves

Preparation
- Cut the corn into bite-sized chunks.
- Cut each cake of bean curd into quarters and then cut each quarter into thin slices. Heat the oil in a wok on medium heat. When the oil is hot, fry the bean curd until golden.
- Remove all but about 2 tablespoonsful of the oil from the wok, add the garlic and stir fry until golden. Add the corn, stir and turn, season to taste with the sugar, soy sauce, seasoning sauce, and salt, and mix well. Slice the spur chillies diagonally, add, stir, and just before removing from the heat, add the basil leaves. When the wok is removed from the heat, stir once again, and then dip onto a serving platter.

Tao-hu Thot Song Khreuang
Fried Bean Curd and Vegetables in Sauce

Ingredients

3-5 tubes soft bean curd, with or without egg
500 grams of a mixture consisting of :
halved ricestraw mushrooms
baby corn cut into one-inch lengths
snow peas with tips and strings removed
green beans with tips and strings removed, cut into one-inch lengths
one-inch lengths of peeled carrot cut into quarters
bite-sized chunks of cauliflower
2 tbsp. coarse textured vegetable protein
3 tbsp. corn flour mixed with water to form a smooth paste
1 tbsp. chopped garlic
2 tbsp. light soy sauce
1/2 tsp. salt
1 tsp. sugar
1 tsp. fermented soybeans
1/4 tsp. pepper
vegetable oil

Preparation

- Cut the bean curd into one-inch-long sections. Heat enough oil to surround the bean curd in a wok on medium heat. When the oil is hot, add the bean curd and fry until golden on one side ; then, turn and fry on the other side. When golden on both sides, remove the bean curd onto a serving platter.
- Remove all but about two tablespoonsful of the oil from the wok. Add the garlic and fry until golden ; then, add the vegetable protein and all the vegetables except the mushrooms. Stir and turn, add the sugar, soy sauce, salt, fermented soybeans, and pepper, and fry with stirring and turning. Add the mushrooms, and when they are tender, pour in enough of the corn flour paste to thicken the liquid and top on the fried bean curd, serve.

Phat Kaphrao Het
Mushrooms Stir-Fried with Chillies and Holy Basil

Phat Phrik Khing
A Savory Companion for Rice

Phat Kaphrao Het
Mushrooms Stir-Fried with Chillies and Holy Basil

Ingredients
300 grams large ricestraw mushrooms
7 yellow chillies
10 cloves garlic
1 tsp. salt
1/2 cup holy basil leaves
2 spur chillies
1/4 cup vegetable oil
1 tbsp. light soy sauce
1 tsp. sugar
3 tbsp. water

Preparation
- Wash the mushrooms and slice off any inedible matter. The mushrooms may then be chopped or cut into thin or thick slices.
- Pound the yellow chillies, garlic, and salt in a mortar until ground and mixed thoroughly.
- Heat the oil in a wok. When hot, stir fry the chilli-garlic mixture until fragrant, add the mushrooms, stir and turn them, and then add the water and cook until the mushrooms are tender.
- Slice the spur chillies diagonally and add them and the basil leaves. Season with soy sauce and sugar, stir well, and then dip onto a serving plate.

Phat Phrik Khing
A Savory Companion for Rice

Ingredients

100 grams coarse textured vegetable protein
100 grams fine textured vegetable protein
1 tbsp. light soy sauce
1/4 cup vegetable oil
1 tbsp. sugar
2 tbsp. finely shredded kaffir lime leaf

Spice Mixture

3 dried chillies
3 cloves garlic
1 tsp. thinly sliced galangal
1/2 tsp. coriander seed
1/2 tsp. chopped coriander root
1 tbsp. thinly sliced shallot
2 tbsp. finely sliced lemon grass
1/2 tsp. sliced kaffir lime rind
1 tsp. salt

Preparation

- Pound the chilli, galangal, kaffir lime rind, and salt in a mortar until well ground ; then, add the rest of the spice mixture ingredients and pound to grind and mix thoroughly.
- Fry the fine and coarse vegetable protein until crisp, remove, and drain.
- Heat the 1/4 cup of oil in a wok. When hot, fry the spice mixture until dried and fragrant, and then season with the sugar and soy sauce to get a salty, sweet, and spicy hot flavor. Now, add the fried vegetable protein and work it around to thoroughly mix with the spices ; then, remove from the heat, allow to stand a minute or two, and then fold in the sliced kaffir lime leaf.

Phat Kaphao Khao Phot
Stir-Fried Corn, Chillies and Holy Basil

190

Phat Phrik Yuak kap Thua Daeng Luang
Stir-Fried Bell Peppers and Kidney Beans

Phat Kaphao Khao Phot
Stir-Fried Corn, Chillies and Holy Basil

Ingredients

2 cups boiled sweet corn kernels
3 yellow chillies
10 cloves garlic
1 tsp. salt
1 tsp. sugar
1/4 cup holy basil leaves
2 spur chillies
1 tbsp. light soy sauce
3 tbsp. vegetable oil

Preparation

- Pound the yellow chillies, garlic, and salt in a mortar until ground and mixed thoroughly.
- Heat the oil in wok. When hot, stir fry the chilli-garlic mixture until fragrant ; then, add the corn and continue stirring and turning.
- Slice the spur chillies diagonally and add together with the basil leaves. Season to taste with the sugar and soy sauce, stir and turn well, and dip onto the serving platter.

Phat Phrik Yuak kap
Thua Daeng Luang
Stir-Fried Bell Peppers and Kidney Beans

Ingredients
3 tbsp. vegetable oil
10 bell peppers
1 cup kidney beans boiled until soft and tender
1/4 cup water
2 tbsp. light soy sauce
2 tsp. dark soy sauce
1 tsp. salt
2 tsp. sugar
1 tbsp. corn flour
3 tbsp. water

Preparation

- Wash the peppers, remove the stems, and cut lengthwise into 1/2-inch wide strips, or cut into quarters.
- Fry the peppers with stirring and turning until they change color . Add the beans, light and dark soy sauces, salt, sugar, and 1/4 cup of water and stir and turn to mix thoroughly.
- Add 3 tbsp. of water to the corn flour and mix to obtain a smooth paste. Add this to the pan, stir well, cook a little while longer, and then dip onto a serving plate.

Phat Tao-hu Khaeng kap Lai Phak
Stir-Fried Bean Curd and Vegetables

Phat Thua Daeng Song Khreuang
Stir-Fried Vegetables with Kidney Beans

Phat Tao-hu Khaeng kap Lai Phak
Stir-Fried Bean Curd and Vegetables

Ingredients
2 cakes firm white bean curd
2 broccoli plants
1 cup coarsely shredded cabbage
1 onion
2 celery plants
1 small bamboo shoot
1 Chinese cabbage
1 cup bean sprouts
2 tbsp. vegetable oil
1 tsp. salt
2 tbsp. light soy sauce
1 tbsp. dark soy sauce
1 tbsp. sugar
1 1/2 tbsp. corn flour
1/4 cup water

Preparation
- Wash the bean curd, cut each cake in half, and then slice each half into pieces about 1/2-cm thick. Wash the broccoli, peel off the tough outer portions of the stems, and then cut the inner portion diagonally into thin slices about 2 inches long. Cut the broccoli curd into small pieces.
- Peel the onion, cut in half top to bottom, and then slice across to obtain half discs about 1/2 cm thick.
- Wash the celery, remove the root, and cut the stems into 1 1/2-inch-long pieces.
- Remove the tough outer portions from the boiled bamboo shoot, slice the shoot in half lengthwise, and then cut each half across into slices about 1/8 inch thick.
- Wash the bean sprouts.
- Wash the Chinese cabbage. Cut the leaves from the stems and cut into 1 1/2-inch lengths.
- Fry the bean curd in 1 tbsp. of the oil. When yellowed,

(See p. 197)

Phat Thua Daeng Song Khreuang
Stir-Fried Vegetables with kidney Bean

Ingredients
2 cups boiled kidney beans
10 yard-long beans cut into 1 1/2-centimeter lengths
3 cloves garlic, chopped
1/4 cup small pieces of tomato
1 cup diced pumpkin
2 tbsp. vegetable oil
1 tbsp. dark soy sauce
1 tsp. salt
3 tbsp. light soy sauce
1 tsp. sugar
1/2 cup water

Preparation
- Marinate the boiled beans in the salt and dark soy sauce.
- Heat the oil in a pan. When hot, add the garlic. As the garlic begins to brown, add the beans and then the pumpkin, stirring and mixing regularly. Add water, light soy sauce and sugar to taste, and then add the tomatoes.
- Serve with rice.

(From p. 196)

remove the curd, add the remaining oil, and then fry the onion until fragrant. Add the bamboo shoot and the broccoli stems, stir with the spatula, and then add the water, light and dark soy sauces, sugar, and salt, and continue to stir and turn.

- When the vegetables in the pan are almost done, add the celery, the shredded cabbage, Chinese cabbage, and broccoli curd and stir with the spatula. Mix the corn flour with 2 tbsp. of water to form a smooth paste, add this to the pan together with the bean sprouts, and stir to mix well. Add the fried bean curd, stir and turn for a short while, and then dip onto a serving platter and sprinkle with pepper.

Phat Jap Chai
Stir-Fried Mixed Vegetables and Bean Curd

Phat Phak Suk Sai Thua Daeng Luang Sai Nga
Stir-Fried Vegetables with Kidney Beans and Sesame

Phat Jap Chai
Stir-Fried Mixed Vegetables and Bean Curd

Ingredients

2 cakes firm white bean curd
25 grams mungbean noodles
100 grams Chinese radish
100 grams Chinese kale, 100 grams celery
100 grams Chinese mustard green
1 small head cabbage, 3 garlic plants
1 small Chinese cabbage, 2 tbsp. chopped garlic
3-4 tbsp. light soy sauce, 3 tbsp. vegetable oil
1 tbsp. dark soy sauce, 1 tsp. sugar
1 tbsp. Seasoning sauce

Preparation

- Slice the bean curd into pieces one inch long and half an inch thick.
- Soak the noodles in water and cut into short lengths.
- Wash and peel the radish, slice in half lengthwise, and then cut into 1-cm-thick slices.
- Wash the kale, peel off the tough skin on the stems, and cut into one-inch lengths. Large diameter stems should be split in half lengthwise. Cut the leaves in half lengthwise and cut across into narrow strips.
- Remove the roots from the celery plants, wash the plants, and cut them into one-inch lengths.
- Cut the cabbage in half and then slice each half into 1 1/2-inch-thick pieces. Remove the roots from the garlic plants, wash the plants, and cut them into one-inch lengths. Wash the Chinese cabbage and cut across into one-inch-thick slices. Wash the Chinese mustard green and cut into one-inch lengths.
- Place the oil in a frying pan and heat. Fry the garlic until fragrant and then add the vegetables in this order, stirring and turning constantly : radish, kale, mustard green, celery, cabbage, garlic plant, Chinese cabbage. Following this, add the bean curd and mungbean noodles.
- Season to taste with light and dark soy sauces, sugar,

(See p. **201**)

Phat Phak Suk Sai Thua Daeng Luang Sai Nga

Stir-Fried Vegetables with Kidney Bean and Sesame

Ingredients

5 boiled yard-long beans
1/2 cup boiled ma-kheua phuang
20 boiled swamp cabbage tips
1 cup scalded bean sprouts
1 cup boiled kidney beans, 3 chillies, 2 shallots
1 garlic bulb, peeled and chopped
1 tsp. salt, 1 tbsp. light soy sauce
2 tbsp. roasted hulled sesame
2 tbsp. vegetable oil

Preparation

- Cut the yard-long bean and the swamp cabbage into 1-cm lengths. Remove the ma-kheua phuang from the stems.
- Pound the chillies and salt well in a mortar. Peel the garlic and the shallots, add to the mortar, and pound. When thoroughly mixed, transfer the paste to a bowl.
- Place the boiled kidney beans in a mortar and break open with the pestle. Add the ma-kheua phuang, break them open, and mix with the bean. Then, add the yard-long bean and break open and mix with the other ingredients with gentle strokes with the pestle.
- Transfer the contents of the mortar to the bowl containing the chilli paste, add the bean sprouts, and gently mix together.
- Fry the garlic in the oil. When fragrant, add the vegetables and the soy sauce and stir and turn until the mixture is hot. Dip into a serving platter and sprinkle with the sesame seeds, which have been broken in a mortar.

(From p. 200)

and seasoning sauce. Continue cooking with regular turning until all the vegetables are tender. Add a little water if the mixture becomes too dry.

Het Hom Op Wun-sen

Shiitake Mushrooms Stewed with Mungbean Noodles

Khai Khao Phot
Corn Omelette

Het Hom Op Wun-sen
Shiitake Mushrooms Stewed with Mungbean Noodles

Ingredients
8-10 shiitake mushrooms
250 grams mungbean noodles
2-3 coriander roots
5 cloves garlic
5 pepper corns, broken
1 tbsp. light soy sauce
2 tsp. seasoning sauce
1/4 tsp. dark soy sauce
10 disc-shapped slices of ginger
3 tbsp. vegetable oil

Preparation
- Soak the noodles in water until supple and then cut into two-inch lengths.
- Wash the mushrooms, soak in water until softened, and if they are large, cut into bite-sized pieces. Retain the water in which the mushrooms were soaked.
- Pound the coriander roots and garlic together in a mortar until finely ground. Heat some oil in a wok, and when hot, add the coriander root-garlic mixture and stir fry until fragrant. Now, add the mushrooms, light soy sauce, seasoning sauce, and the water in which the mushrooms were soaked. Allow the mixture to come to a boil ; then, remove from the heat and set aside.
- Put the 3 tbsp. of oil in a heavy pot. Arrange the discs of ginger on the bottom and then the noodles. Pour the fried mushroom mixture evenly over the noodles and sprinkle with the pepper and the dark soy sauce.
- Cover and place on low heat for a few minutes ; then, increase to medium heat and cook slowly for about 30 minutes until the noodles are tender.

Khai Khao Phot
Corn Omelette

Ingredients

3 eggs
2 ears corn
1 tbsp. minced garlic
2 tbsp. light soy sauce
1/4 tsp. pepper
3 tbsp. vegetable oil

Preparation

- Cut the kernels of corn from the cob in thin slices.
- Break the eggs into a bowl, add the soy sauce and pepper, beat well, add the corn, and stir to mix thoroughly.
- Heat the oil in a wok until very hot over medium heat. Then, pour the egg mixture into the wok so as to form a disc. Fry until the egg is golden on one side, turn over and fry until golden on the other side, and then place on a serving dish.

Khai Jiao Na Noei Khaeng lae Man Farang
Cheese and Potato Omelette

Phat Phak Mangsawirat
Stir-Fried Vegetables

207

Khai Jiao Na Noei Khaeng lae Man Farang
Cheese and Potato Omelette

Ingredients

4 eggs
3 tbsp. margarine or butter
1/4 cup chopped roasted peanuts
1/2 cup one-half-centimeter cubes of potato
1/4 cup chopped onion
2 tbsp. grated cheese
1 tbsp. chopped celery
1 tsp. salt
1/4 cup yoghurt

Preparation

- Melt 1 1/2 tbsp. of the margarine or butter in a frying pan over low heat. Add the onion add the potato and fry, turning and stirring regularly, until the potato is cooked ; then, transfer to a dish and set aside.

- Beat the eggs. Melt the remaining margarine or butter in a broad, shallow frying pan over low heat. Pour the egg into the pan and then add the yoghurt. As the egg becomes firm, slide it about in the pan using the spatula and at the same time move the pan about so that whole interior surface of the pan is coated with egg.

- Sprinkle the egg with the grated cheese, then with the onion and potato. Sprinkle with the peanut, salt and celery. When the egg is firm, cut like a pie into wedge-shaped pieces and then transfer to a serving platter.

Phat Phak Mangsawirat
Stir-Fried Vegetables

Ingredients

**3-4 dried shiitake mushrooms, soaked in water
and sliced crossways
(save the water used for soaking the mushrooms)
100 grams abalone mushrooms sliced crossways
100 grams ricestraw mushrooms cut in half
100 grams baby corn sliced diagonally
100 grams cauliflower cut into chunks
100 grams cabbage cut into large slices
50 grams sugar peas, tips of the pod and strings removed
50 grams bean sprouts, hulls and root tips removed
1/2 tsp. salt
1 tbsp. light soy sauce
1/2 tsp. sugar
1 tbsp. coarsely chopped garlic
1/4 cup vegetable oil**

Preparation

- Heat the oil in a wok. When hot, add the garlic, and when it is golden, add the shiitake mushroom and the cauliflower and stir fry until tender.
- Then, add the abalone mushroom, ricestraw mushroom, corn, cabbage, and sugar peas, and the salt, soy sauce, and sugar, and a little of the water in which the shiitake mushrooms were soaked. Stir well. When the liquid comes to a boil, add the bean sprouts, stir and turn to mix well, and dip up onto a serving platter.